GREAT EMPIRES OF THE PAST

Empire of Alexander the Great

DEBRA SKELTON AND PAMELA DELL

☑®

Facts On File, Inc.

Great Empires of the Past: EMPIRE OF ALEXANDER THE GREAT

History Consultant: Eugene N. Borza, emeritus professor of ancient history, Pennsylvania State University

Facts On File, Inc.
132 West 31st Street
New York NY 10001

Library of Congress Cataloging-in-Publication Data
Skelton, Debra.
Empire of Alexander the Great / Debra Skelton and Pamela Dell.
p. cm.
Includes bibliographical references and index.
ISBN 0-8160-5564-5 (HC)
1. Greece–History–Macedonian Expansion, 359-323 B.C. 2. Alexander, the Great, 356-323 B.C. I. Dell, Pamela. II. Title.
DF234.S58 2005
930'.0971238–dc22   2004056430

Facts On File books are available at special discounts when purchased in bulk quantities for businesses, associations, institutions, or sales promotions. Please call our Special Sales Department in New York at (212) 967-8800 or (800) 322-8755.

You can find Facts On File on the World Wide Web at http://www.factsonfile.com

Produced by the Shoreline Publishing Group LLC
Editorial Director: James Buckley Jr.
Series Editor: Beth Adelman
Designed by Thomas Carling, Carling Design, Inc.
Photo research by Dawn Friedman, Bookmark Publishing
Index by Nanette Cardon, IRIS

Photo and art credits: The Art Archive/Archaeological Museum Istanbul/Dagli Orti: 1,14; Museo Archeologico Nazionale, Naples, Italy/Bridgeman Art Library: 3, 40;Corporation of London/Topham-HIP/The Image Works: 4; Gianni Dagli Orti/Corbis: 6, 16; Erich Lessing/Art Resource: NY: 12, 34, 91, 96; North Wind Picture Archives: 22, 98; The Granger Collection, New York: 23, 26; Hulton Archive/Getty Images: 28, 48; Giraudon/Art Resource, NY: 30; Reza, Webistan/Corbis: 36; Facts On File: 44, 119; Bibliotheque Municipale, Reims, France, Giraudon/Bridgeman Art Library: 51; The Art Archive/Museo del Prado Madrid/Dagli Orti (A): 56; Musee de la Ville de Paris, Musee du Petit-Palais, France, Lauros/Giraudon/Bridgeman Art Library: 59; Narodni Muzej, Belgrade, Serbia, Lauros/Giraudon/Bridgeman Art Library: 64; Bettmann/Corbis: 67; Scala/Art Resource, NY: 68, 75; The Art Archive/Archaeological Museum Salonica/Dagli Orti (A): 78; The Art Archive/Museo Capitolino Rome/Dagli Orti: 85; SEF/Art Resource, NY: 87; Atta Kenare/AFP/Getty Images: 95; The Pierpont Morgan Library/Art Resource, NY: 102; Victoria & Albert Museum, London/Art Resource, NY: 107; Warner Brothers/Courtesy Everett Collection: 112; Srdjan Ilic/AP/Wide World Photos: 116

Printed in the United States of America

VB PKG 10 9 8 7 6 5 4 3 2 1

This book is printed on acid-free paper.

CONTENTS

ALEXANDER THE GREAT

J.S. Westmacott Sculp^t 1863.

Introduction

IN 336 B.C.E., A PROUD, INTELLIGENT, AND SUPREMELY ambitious young man rose to the throne of Macedonia, a kingdom on the northern border of modern-day Greece. Only 20 years old, he was already bristling to rule the mighty Persian Empire to the east. The fact that he accomplished this feat and much more, despite the wealth, power, and, often, the huge military strength of his foes—and in just under 12 years—illustrates his extraordinary gifts as a leader and military strategist. It has also kept his name in the forefront of legendary "action figures" even into the 21st century, more than 2,300 years later. He is still known throughout the world as Alexander the Great.

Born to Greatness

Alexander III of Macedon (356–323 B.C.E.) was the son of King Philip II of Macedon (382–336 B.C.E.) and Olympias of Epirus (c. 376–316 B.C.E.) (in what is now modern-day Albania), daughter of King Neoptolemus I. Alexander's birth, which some historians say probably occurred in the month of July, was accompanied by various unusual events. One of these was the burning down of the Temple of Artemis, the goddess of the wilderness, wild animals, and the hunt. Soothsayers (those who foretold the future based on signs) consulted by King Philip prophesied that these events indicated his son's great destiny. Whether or not the prophecies were legitimate, the fact remains that Alexander became the most successful warrior in the history of the world.

From the age of 20 until his death at only 32, Alexander and his armies swept across a vast region that included Persia, Asia Minor, Syria, and Egypt. He traveled thousands of miles with his troops and ultimately ruled an empire that stretched approximately 2 million square miles over three continents. In his conquest of the known world, he overcame armies far more powerful than his by being smarter, more resourceful, and more determined than his enemies.

One consequence of this conquest was that the culture of Greece, over which Alexander also ruled, was introduced into Egypt and Asia, altering the course of history. The spread of Greek culture, government, language, art, and ideas laid the groundwork for civilizations that continue to this day.

After Alexander's death, his huge empire quickly fell apart, but his legendary status increased as tales of his deeds were told, passed down, and retold. His life was instructional for many other great conquerors and rulers as well, including Julius Caesar, Queen Cleopatra VII, and Napoleon Bonaparte.

The young prince had the best possible background for someone with great ambitions. King Philip II was an aggressive leader who set an example for his son by conquering neighboring lands when Alexander was just an infant. As he grew up, Alexander spent much of his childhood among the soldiers of his father's army. Another important influence on the young prince was his teacher Aristotle (384–322 B.C.E.), one of the greatest Greek philosophers ever to have lived. Aristotle, who wrote or edited several hundred books, taught the young prince geography, botany, zoology, logic, and many other subjects.

Greek Decline

Alexander came of age just after the so-called Golden Age of Greek civilization, which was at its height between 500 and 400 B.C.E. The Greeks were renowned as statesmen, philosophers, builders, poets, dramatists, and sculptors.

But by the time Alexander was born, Greek civilization had begun to decline. Even so, the Greeks were justifiably proud of their knowledge, language, and refinement, and their customs and ideas still had powerful influence in the world. They thought very highly of themselves–and not so highly

Like Father, Like Son
Philip II was an aggressive leader who set a bold example for his son. This sculpture was made around 350 to 390 B.C.E.

of their neighbors to the north, the Macedonians. In fact, although the Macedonian kings claimed that the royal family was descended from the Greek heroes Heracles and Achilles, for the most part the Greeks considered the Macedonians to be uncivilized barbarians living on the fringes of Greece. But these tough frontiersmen became effective soldiers under the leadership of Philip II.

At the time, Greece was divided into many separate city-states, each of which had its own army. Some of them relied on mercenaries (paid soldiers) for protection. The city-states often fought among themselves. Philip took advantage of this disunity by taking control of the Greek city-states one by one, through a combination of diplomacy and force. Eventually, Philip's success transformed the minor kingdom of Macedonia into a dominant power that ruled all of Greece. His son later surpassed this surprising military and political achievement by making Macedonia, for a brief time, the most powerful kingdom in the world.

Ancient Super Heroes

Alexander and his friends did not have any comic books, television, or movies, but they did have super heroes. They read the accounts of their heroes' brave deeds primarily in *The Iliad*, an epic poem written by Greek poet Homer centuries before Alexander's birth. (The dates of Homer's life are not known, but he lived in the ninth or eighth century B.C.E.) In that book, Homer tells the exciting story of the Greeks' siege of Troy and the beautiful Helen, who inspired that battle, the legendary Trojan War.

The battles of great warriors and princes such as Achilles, Hector, Paris, and others, many of whom were believed to be descended directly from the Greek gods, may have inspired Alexander. In fact, the young king loved *The Iliad* so much that he memorized most of its 16,000 lines and used these super warriors as role models for his own life and values. He even slept with a copy of *The Iliad* under his pillow—right next to his dagger.

Alexander in Charge

When Alexander was only 16 years old, his father named him as regent, or temporary ruler, of Macedonia while he was away for an extended period of time. When Thrace, one of the Macedonian colonies, revolted, Alexander quickly marched troops to the area. He conquered the rebels and renamed their stronghold Alexandroupolis. It was to become the first of several cities that he founded and named after himself.

In 338 B.C.E., at the age of 18, Alexander led the left flank of the Macedonian cavalry (soldiers who fight on horseback) in the battle of Chaeronea, northwest of Athens. This decisive battle crushed the final Greek resistance to Philip's rule. Two years later, in July of 336 B.C.E.,

Alexander became king of Macedonia after Philip was murdered by one of his bodyguards. Many historians have speculated that Alexander's ambitious and ruthless mother, Queen Olympias, conspired in the plot against his father, but no factual evidence of this has been uncovered.

Philip's Greek "allies," who had been forced to recognize him as their leader, saw his death—and his heir's youth and inexperience—as an opportunity to reclaim their independence. When, in 335 B.C.E., Alexander turned his attention to fighting a group of tribes in the north who were rebelling against Macedonia, two of the more southern Greek city-states, Thebes and Athens, began their own uprising. Alexander immediately swept into Greece with his troops to assert his leadership. He offered to negotiate peace with the two city-states. When Thebes refused, the young king burned down the ancient city, sparing only its temple, killed its soldiers, and sold some 30,000 of its citizens into slavery. Athens quickly surrendered and Alexander spared that ancient city-state. Treating those who surrendered with clemency remained his usual practice for much of his life.

Alexander convinced the Greek city-states to appoint him as leader of the League of Corinth, a governing council established by his father a year before his death. The League members had appointed Philip to lead an invasion of the Persian Empire. They now agreed to put Alexander in charge of that invasion.

Ancient Enemy

The Persian Empire was Greece's neighbor to the east. This vast empire, which stretched from Egypt and the Mediterranean to India and central Asia, had dominated the ancient world for more than two centuries. It was the wealthiest and most powerful nation in the Middle East, and a long-standing enemy of Greece—with good reason. The Persians, in an attempt to expand their empire, had started a series of wars of conquest with Greece that began in about 500 B.C.E.

Before Alexander's time, Persian kings had been great warriors, but success had made them somewhat lazy and complacent. Their vast wealth remained, but their power was waning. In 334 B.C.E., after two years of preparation, Alexander began to put into motion the plan his father had made before his death—the invasion of the Persian Empire. He was so confident victory would be swift that Alexander set out for Persia with only enough money, borrowed from the Macedonian treasury, to pay a single month's salary to his army. He expected to meet such expenses thereafter with the riches of the Persian Empire.

WHAT ARE CONNECTIONS?

Throughout this book, and all the books in the Great Empires of the Past series, you will find Connections boxes. They point out ideas, inventions, art, food, customs, and more from this empire that are still part of our world today. Nations and cultures in remote history can seem far removed from our world, but these connections demonstrate how our everyday lives have been shaped by the peoples of the past.

Over the next three years, Alexander won three major battles against the Persians. During each of these battles he was greatly outnumbered, but through quick thinking, brilliant tactics and strategy, and bravery, he was able to exploit his enemy's weaknesses. In both of the last two of the battles, the tide started to turn against Darius III (380–330 B.C.E.), the Great King of Persia, and he fled the battlefield. After the third battle, some of his officers murdered Darius. For some it was part of the struggle to replace him, and for others an attempt to gain favor with Alexander.

Best known as a great warrior, Alexander also had the makings of a strong leader, although he never had a chance to rule the lands he conquered. Although many Greeks considered the Persians inferior barbarians, he believed them to be the equals of the Macedonians and honored their customs and religions.

Everywhere Alexander and his army went, they established new garrison towns. He often appointed Persians friendly to him as local rulers, or allowed existing Persian rulers to remain in charge. He also explored ways to achieve harmony and equality between his soldiers and the newly conquered Persians. One way he attempted to bring this about was by organizing a mass marriage ceremony, in which he and about 90 of his officers married Persian women.

The End of the Road

Alexander is considered by many to be the greatest general who ever lived, not only because of his military genius, but also because of his ability to inspire and motivate his men. This inspiration came from many sources. Alexander was one of the last great commanders in history to lead battles in person. Risking his safety in this way, he suffered many of the same wounds as his soldiers. He treated his soldiers exceptionally well and knew many of them personally. He was also an incredibly charismatic leader.

Nevertheless, the long years away from home and the hardships the troops experienced took a toll. During the 12 years of Alexander's reign, he and his army crisscrossed the Persian Empire, traveling 20,000 miles—a distance about six times wider than the United States—across rugged mountain ranges, raging rivers, and scorching deserts, on foot and on horseback. They conquered everything in their path, never losing a major battle.

Finally, Alexander led his troops into India, and they began conquering this country from the northeastern border of the Persian Empire. But after months of steady rain and physical hardship, the soldiers had had enough. They realized their leader was never going to willingly stop

INTELLIGENCE GATHERING

There is no way of knowing what Alexander dreamed of when he was a boy, because no personal records survive. But later writers often invented stories about him that claimed his desire to rule the world burned within him almost from birth. These stories eventually became widespread and were widely believed. One such story said that even as a boy Alexander may have been planning for the war with Persia; when Persian dignitaries visited his father's court, the young prince questioned them at length about Persia's army, roads, communications, and customs.

fighting and refused to continue on with him—which was their right under Macedonian law.

Alexander reluctantly headed back to Persia, and it is doubtful that he intended ever to return to Macedonia. He reached Babylon (in what is now Iraq) in April 323 B.C.E. , and died there about two months later, in mid-June 323 B.C.E. He was 32 years old. Rumors circulated in ancient times that he was poisoned, but modern scholars believe he died of an infectious disease, probably typhoid fever. About 13 years after Alexander's death, his wife Roxane and son Alexander IV, who was born shortly after his death, were both murdered.

In 12 years, Alexander had conquered more lands and extended his leadership farther than any European ruler. He and his troops brought Greek culture, language, and ideas to these distant lands. Long after his death, Greek culture continued to influence the development of many civilizations west of the Tigris-Euphrates Valley.

The Man vs. the Legend

Alexander the Great is a fascinating figure. Historians and scholars continue to write books and make movies about him, and each writer puts his or her own interpretation on their renowned subject, making it difficult to know exactly who he really was. No documents from Alexander's time have survived; all existing accounts of his deeds were written after his death. Many accounts contain conflicting information, making it even more difficult to know the truth about many of the events of his life.

Scholars have cast the great conqueror in shades of both dark and light. Many consider Alexander an enlightened leader because he believed in the peaceful co-existence of different peoples within his empire and tried to improve the quality of life in the lands he conquered. He is considered a visionary by some because of his belief that people should see themselves as part of a global kingdom that includes every human being, rather than as belonging just to their own nation.

Others emphasize Alexander's very real darker side. Some historians have perceived him to be a violent drunkard. They point to the facts that he destroyed some of the cities he conquered, had women and children sold into slavery, and once killed a close friend in a drunken rage. The Macedonians reportedly used brutal force to subdue some of the people they conquered, even butchering the sick and elderly in some places. Some historians see Alexander as an egotistical tyrant, who began to consider himself a god and demanded that his troops and subjects worship him. He even claimed the status of god for his warhorse, Bucephalas, naming a city in India after him.

Nearly all historians agree that Alexander was bisexual, pointing to his close lifelong relationship with his comrade Hephaestion. Homosexuality and bisexuality were accepted practices in ancient Greece and Macedonia, and did not have the stigma in that culture that they have in many places today. In the Middle Ages, Alexander was portrayed as a legendary hero who followed the knights' code of chivalry, the ideal of bravery and honor. In modern Iran, his image is that of a villain—the personification of the devil. In trying to understand this complex personality, however, it is important to keep in mind the culture of his time, in which hard drinking and bisexuality were accepted practices, as was waging war, conquering territory, and enslaving enemies.

Historians, scholars, and military experts do agree on some things. Alexander was an extremely charismatic leader with an incredibly powerful personality. They also agree that he was one of the most outstanding generals of all time. By conquering nearly the entire known world of his era, he accomplished more at a younger age, and in fewer years, than most people do in a lifetime.

Alexander's Legacy: Hellenistic Civilization

Alexander's conquests changed the character of the world so much that historians divide history into two distinct periods: before and after his reign. The classical, or Hellenic, period of Greek history is considered by most historians to have ended with Alexander's death in 323 B.C.E. The Greek city-states never regained their former greatness, but their culture continued to spread far and wide. Thus, the post-Alexander era of civilization, distinct from the earlier Hellenic age, is known as the Hellenistic period.

During Alexander's lifetime and before, the people usually referred to in English as "the Greeks" called themselves Hellenes. Though they were mostly found within the borders of today's nation of Greece, the Hellenes did not identify themselves by the area they lived in so much as by their Hellenic language (ancient Greek). Anyone who spoke Hellenic was considered an Hellene.

For nearly 300 years after Alexander's death, Greek (or Hellenistic) language, art, and culture flourished throughout the Middle East. The last Hellenistic ruler was the Egyptian queen Cleopatra VII (b. 69 B.C.E.). She was the last of a long line of Macedonian rulers of Egypt, and her death in 30 B.C.E. marks the end of the Hellenistic period.

THE MAKING OF A MYTH

Many books about Alexander were based on *The Romance of Alexander the Great,* an account that is thought to have been written in about 200 c.e. by an author who came to be known as Pseudo-Callisthenes. Pseudo-Callisthenes was an unknown poet, probably of the third century, who falsely ascribed his work to Callisthenes (d. 327 B.C.E), the nephew of Aristotle and one of Alexander's original biographers. Psuedo-Callisthenes' book was based on oral and written legends that were passed down after Alexander's death. The following description of Alexander's birth (as quoted in *Alexander and His Times* by Frederic Theule) shows the exaggeration and embellishment that was typical of many of these early writings:

> "... the newborn fell to the ground; there was a flash of lightning, thunder resounded, the earth trembled, and the whole world shook."

Hellenistic Influence

This altar to the Roman god Zeus is a classic example of Hellenistic architecture. It was built around 180 B.C.E. in Pergamon (modern Bergama in Turkey). It was taken to Germany in 1871 and is currently exhibited at the Pergamon Museum in Berlin.

The enlargement of the Greek world had far-reaching consequences and became Alexander's most lasting legacy. Before his reign, world civilization was dominated by Eastern cultures, in particular Persian, Egyptian, and Babylonian. Because of Alexander's conquests, his culture and the most significant aspects of Greek society permeated both East and West, and Europe in particular. Greek politics, language, learning, culture, art, and ideas affected the way many civilizations subsequently developed.

Hellenism can be considered the world's first great economic boom. Huge areas opened up to world trade and development. New industries and agricultural ventures flourished. Enormous amounts of money entered into circulation because Alexander began minting coins from the silver and gold reserves of the Persian kings, who had hoarded their vast wealth for centuries. The system of economics and trade that began with Alexander remained basically the same for the next 2,000 years, until the Industrial Revolution of the 19th century.

Hellenism changed the course of history and continues to shape culture worldwide. Even today it remains a major influence on our own language, customs, government, design, and architecture. This probably would not have happened were it not for the huge ambition of a single Macedonian man.

PART I

HISTORY

The Beginning of Alexander's Empire

The Empire at Its Largest

Final Years of the Empire

CHAPTER 1

The Beginning of Alexander's Empire

WHEN ALEXANDER BECAME KING OF MACEDONIA IN 336 B.C.E., he inherited one of the greatest armies in the world. His father, Philip, was an extremely powerful king who laid the groundwork for Alexander's remarkable accomplishments. When Philip came to power in 359 B.C.E., Macedonia was a poor country with a feudal society. Once established as ruler, he began a systematic policy of unifying and expanding his kingdom. During the 23 years of his rule, he turned Macedonia into a world power. He developed Macedonia's mining, trade, and agriculture. He transformed a poor and backward country into a united and powerful state, bringing Greece under Macedonian rule as well.

Philip also established a very well-trained permanent army, making the military a full-time occupation and way of life for many Macedonian men. Before this time, soldiering had been a part-time job. Most men worked as farmers during most of the year and were able to pick up some extra money as soldiers when they were not needed on the farm. They would then return to their farms at the start of the harvest. Under Philip, the military paid well enough to enable men to be soldiers year-round. This meant Philip could drill his army regularly, and much time and effort was spent on maneuvers, which built discipline and unity among the troops. Philip's military reforms and conquests helped establish this professional fighting force and created a sense of national pride among the Macedonians.

For some time, Philip had been preparing for an attack on the Persian Empire. The Persians had invaded Greece 150 years earlier, destroying many temples and other important buildings, and still ruled several eastern Greek cities they had conquered. This neighbor was a constant threat to the Greeks, and in 337 B.C.E., under Philip's influence, the

OPPOSITE
The Conqueror
A scene from the relief carved on a sarcophagus (stone coffin) shows a battle between Alexander the Great and the Persians. It was made in the late 4th century B.C.E. in Sidon, Libya.

Macedonian Armor
King Philip II's body armor is made of iron and decorated with gold. This piece dates from about 350 B.C.E. and was found in Philip's tomb in Vergina, Greece.

Greeks agreed to declare war on their enemy to the east.

The closest part of the Persian Empire to Greece was Asia Minor (which means "lesser Asia"). It is a broad peninsula that lies between the Black and Mediterranean Seas, and corresponds roughly to what is today the country of Turkey. From there, the empire stretched east to the deserts of present-day Iran in the east, to India in the southeast, and to Egypt in the southwest.

As the supreme commander of the Panhellenic, or combined Greek and Macedonian forces, Philip sent about 10,000 soldiers to attack the coast of Asia Minor in the spring of 336 B.C.E. His plan was to join this expeditionary force and lead the charge into Persia. But with his assassination, this task fell to Alexander.

Alexander was ready to take up the throne, and Philip had certainly set the stage for his son, but Alexander's successes were entirely his own. Making use of the army his father had created, he extended the power, wealth, and influence of Macedonia and Greece farther than Philip probably ever dreamed possible.

Victory Begins at Home

Before Alexander could carry forward his father's plans to attack Persia, he had to spend about two years getting control of matters at home. Some of the tribes from Thrace, along Macedonia's northern frontier, rebelled after Philip's death. While Alexander was away fighting them, two of the major Greek city-states, Athens and Thebes, decided it would be a good time to shake off Macedonian rule. Bribed by King Darius III of Persia, they too rebelled.

The two city-states had underestimated the young king. Alexander quickly descended into Thebes with his army and demanded surrender. When the Thebans refused, Alexander's soldiers burned down the city and sold its citizens into slavery as a warning to other Greeks who were considering rebellion. The warning did not go unheeded by Athens, which quickly surrendered. Alexander, whose respect for the once-great center of Greek culture continued for the rest of his life, accepted Athens's surrender and did not destroy the city or punish its citizens.

Alexander now prepared to carry out his father's plans to attack the Persian Empire. The official reasons given by both Alexander and his father for this attack were to avenge the Persians' destruction of Greek temples and other precious buildings, and to liberate the Greek cities of Asia Minor. The real purpose, however, may have been the need for money. Although Philip had greatly increased Macedonia's wealth, some historians believe the kingdom was on the verge of bankruptcy. With Persia's rulers weaker than they had ever been, it was a good time to take control of this wealthy enemy. Alexander also wanted to win his own fame.

In the early spring of 334 B.C.E., borrowing enough money from the Macedonian treasury to keep his troops supplied for a month, Alexander left Macedonia with an army of about 30,000 infantry, or foot soldiers, and 5,000 cavalry, or mounted horsemen. The army was made up of Macedonians as well as troops drawn from throughout Greece and from the Balkan lands to the north. Alexander left trusted generals behind, with enough soldiers to keep the peace in Macedonia and Greece.

Traveling an average of 20 miles a day, Alexander and his troops reached the Hellespont in 20 days. Crossing this narrow strip of water between Europe and Asia, they landed in Persian territory, in what is today Turkey. Upon his arrival, Alexander visited the ruins of Troy. Through his familiarity with Homer's *The Iliad* and its legendary tales of those he believed to be his ancestors (see page 7), the young monarch was well aware of Troy's history. It was the site of the first Greek invasion of Asia, about 900 years before Alexander's time. Now he came to conquer again.

At Troy, Alexander made a sacrifice at what local legend said was the grave of the Greek hero Achilles. He also dedicated his army to the Greek goddess Athena, who, in times of war, was worshiped as the goddess of intelligence and cunning. He was ready to take on the Persians.

The Battle of Granicus

Between 334 and 331 B.C.E., Alexander won three decisive battles against the Persian Empire. The first of these was at the Granicus River (today Kocabas Cay in Turkey) in May of 334 B.C.E. Darius III was so disrespectful of his young foe that he did not come to the battlefield at all. Instead, he sent the local satrap, or regional governor, and a force of Persian cavalry and Greek mercenaries to turn back the invaders.

TATTOOED "BARBARIANS"

One of Macedonia's long-standing enemies was Thrace, its neighbor to the north. The Macedonians thought of the Thracians as forest tribes of tattooed barbarians who dressed in fox skins. Certainly, they were nothing like the well-organized, well-equipped, and well-trained soldiers the Macedonians would later fight in Persia. Some Thracians became soldiers in Alexander's army.

The Persian troops met Alexander's forces at the river. The Persians held a strong position, lined up along the eastern bank of the Granicus, but Darius's commanders made a fatal error. They had positioned their cavalry in front and their infantry in back, the standard defensive formation of the Persian army. Alexander, always shrewd in the heat of battle, quickly saw that this formation would keep the Persian cavalry boxed in and unable to maneuver easily. The Macedonian king attacked at once, even though it was late in the afternoon; he feared that if he waited, the Persians might realize their mistake and reorganize their troops. Alexander himself led the charge of the main cavalry, sending his infantry directly across the river. The Macedonians had to cross the deep, rapid river and climb the steep banks of the Granicus to attack.

There was savage fighting. Alexander was injured and lay unconscious for a short time as the battle raged around him. He regained consciousness, got back on his horse, Bucephalas, and charged into the center of the enemy troops. Soon, the Macedonians had gained the upper hand. As the frantic Persians retreated, many men were trampled by their fleeing comrades. The Macedonians butchered the Persian soldiers. They were especially brutal toward the Greek mercenaries who fought for the Persians (whom they viewed as traitors), hacking them into pieces. About 2,000 Greek mercenaries survived the battle. They were shipped back to Macedonia to work in the mines as slaves.

Alexander lost only about 150 soldiers at Granicus. He buried them with military honors and promised to pay their debts back home. He also excused their families from paying taxes in the future. The victory at Granicus opened Asia Minor to Alexander and his army. As they marched south along the Aegean Sea, many cities that had previously been conquered by the Persian Empire welcomed them as liberators, turning over their treasuries without hesitation. He became even more popular as his generous treatment of those who surrendered became widely known.

CONNECTIONS >>>>>>>>>>>>>

Traces in Thrace

After his victory at Granicus, Alexander laid a brutal sentence on the captured Greek mercenaries who had fought against him in that battle. They were sent, disgraced and in chains, back to Thrace, the ancient territory bounded by Macedonia on the southwest and the Danube River on the north. These unfortunate mercenaries lived out the rest of their lives doing hard labor in the silver mines there. Some of their manacled (handcuffed) skeletons have been found in Thrace by modern-day archaeologists.

After the battle at Granicus, Alexander saw the wisdom of capturing Persia's coastal cities before driving deeper into the country. The Persians had a powerful fleet of warships, and he did not have the naval strength to defeat them at sea. As long as the Persian fleet sailed the Mediterranean, they would remain a threat. Alexander realized that by capturing key ports that supplied the Persian ships with food and water, the navy would eventually have to surrender. He also needed to control the ports in order to ship reinforcements and supplies to his army.

The coastal city of Miletus resisted, and a Persian fleet of 400 ships with 80,000 men headed there to reinforce the city. Alexander's brilliant solution was simply to blockade the harbor, so the Persian ships could not bring their troops ashore. Miletus fell quickly. But Alexander was so impressed by the courage of the Greek mercenaries who fought there that, unlike earlier battles, he accepted them into his army.

Alexander used the same technique along the east coast of the Aegean Sea. This kept the Persian fleet from being able to get fresh water and supplies. Despite its huge size, Persia's mighty navy was defeated, simply because Alexander's army managed to capture so many coastal cities. About a year and a half after Alexander's first onslaught, the entire Persian fleet surrendered.

The Battle of Issus

By 333 B.C.E., Alexander reached the coast of Syria. In October of that year, in a fierce battle at Issus (a coastal plain between what is now Turkey and Syria), the Macedonians had their second major encounter with the Persian army. This time, Darius was there to lead his troops into battle.

The Persians outnumbered the Macedonians, but once again they made a deadly mistake. They chose to fight on a narrow plain bordered by the sea, a river, and mountains. Alexander ordered his infantry to charge into a heavy shower of arrows. With his personal regiment, the Companion cavalry, he charged directly into the Persian lines and broke them up—they had no room to maneuver around the Macedonian charge.

The Macedonians quickly overwhelmed the Persians. The Persians lost an estimated 100,000 soldiers at Issus. Only about 450 Macedonians are believed to have been killed. Darius fled, followed by many of his men. He left behind his chariot and royal cloak and abandoned a fortune in gold. He also abandoned his mother, wife, and daughters in a royal tent that was set up behind the battlefield—a tent more luxurious than anything the Macedonians had ever seen. Alexander surprised the Persians by treating

IMMORTAL SOLDIERS
Persia's King Darius III had a personal bodyguard of 10,000 soldiers. These specially chosen soldiers were called The Immortals, because when a soldier was killed, a new recruit immediately replaced him.

his royal hostages as honored guests instead of killing them—as was the custom of the time. Over time, he even developed an extremely close relationship with Darius's mother, Sisygambis. That relationship continued until the end of his life.

The Siege of Tyre

Alexander now marched south through Phoenicia (a territory that now roughly comprises the coastal area of Lebanon). The major port cities of Sidon and Byblos (now Jubayl in Lebanon) surrendered to him without a fight, but when Alexander arrived at the fortified island of Tyre in February 332 B.C.E., the city refused to let him enter. A walled fortress off the coast of what is now Lebanon, Tyre was a strategic coastal base, and Alexander knew he had to capture it. But gaining control of the island city would prove to be his most difficult military operation so far.

Tyre lay about a half mile off the mainland. The water surrounding it was about 18 feet deep, and its walls were about 150 feet high. Its harbor was well fortified and there was no land beyond the city walls. Alexander

CONNECTIONS >>>>>>>>>>>>>>>>>>>>>>>>>>>>>>>>

A Knotty Problem

Alexander's smallest conquest has become one of his most famous. In 333 B.C.E., before the battle of Issus, he entered the city of Gordium in what is now Turkey. There he encountered the already legendary Gordian knot. In the local temple of Zeus sat a wagon that legend said belonged to King Gordius, the father of Midas. Holding the wagon's yoke to its shaft was this Gordian knot, a complex, tightly-woven mass whose undetectable ends were buried deep within the knot itself.

An ancient prophecy said that the person who untied the Gordian knot would become the ruler of Asia. Many had attempted this task but no one had been able to so much as loosen the knot—not even Alexander the Great—because of its unfathomable intricacy. But Alexander, unlike the others, refused to accept failure.

As usual, there is more than one account of what happened when the young conqueror confronted the knot. But according to the most dramatic tales, Alexander, in typically aggressive fashion, ultimately slashed through it with one powerful hack of his sword. And he did indeed go on to fulfill the Gordian prophecy.

Today, the term *Gordian knot* is still in our vocabulary; it means an especially complicated and difficult problem whose solution does not seem obvious.

decided to lay siege to Tyre–a military move in which the army surrounds and blockades a city in an attempt to starve out its residents. He hired thousands of local workers to help the Macedonian soldiers build a mole–a massive land bridge–that reached from the mainland to the island. To build this causeway, they used debris from the old city of Tyre, by then an abandoned ruin on the mainland. They drove wooden piles into the seabed to support the mole and piled rocks and logs on top. The work was extremely difficult and dangerous, and the Tyrians did not make it any easier. They used catapults to hurl stones and balls of burning debris at their enemies, and shot arrows at them. They captured some of the Macedonians and slaughtered them, then tossed them into the sea in view of their comrades. But Alexander's men, using screens and shields to protect themselves, continued building the mole.

When they finally finished, the mole was about half a mile long and 200 feet wide. Unfortunately for the Macedonians, the wall where the land bridge came ashore was too strong for them to batter down. But at the same time the mole was being built, Alexander also constructed several 150-foot portable wooden towers, or siege towers, which were covered with iron plates to make them fireproof. Battering rams, catapults, or siege engines–machines that throw a projectile–were then mounted on these towers.

Alexander also commandeered about 120 ships from the nearby city of Sidon, and mounted siege engines on their decks. In August 332 B.C.E., these ships moved in to attack Tyre from both north and south. The Tyrians piled rocks in the water around their island to keep the ships from drawing near, used their catapults to fling enormous boulders in hopes of sinking the ships, and poured scalding liquids and red-hot sand on them.

The Tyrians held out for seven months against Alexander's siege, but eventually were defeated. Alexander and his men destroyed most of the city, massacred more than 8,000 Tyrians, and sold the remaining 30,000 residents into slavery. This slaughter was intended as punishment for the

Siege Towers

Among the innovative weapons used by the Macedonian army were siege towers that could be taken apart and put back together in different shapes. According to *Library of History* by Diodorus Siculus, each floor of the 60-foot wood and metal towers "... had two stairways, one to bring up the material and the other one to go down, so that all the servicing was done without disorder. And 3,400 people, chosen for their strength, were in charge of moving the machine, all of them pushing at the same time, some from the interiors, others from behind and the sides," (as quoted in *Alexander and His Times*, by Frederic Theule).

Tearing Down the Walls
Large catapults like this one that flung barrels of burning material, and innovative siege towers enabled Alexander's army to effectively attack walled cities.

way the Tyrians had treated Macedonian prisoners, as well as a warning to other cities.

Onward to Egypt

After his victory at Tyre, Alexander headed for Egypt, the richest part of the Persian Empire. Its farms grew the best wheat and fruit in all the Mediterranean lands, and its ancient culture was widely admired. The Egyptians welcomed Alexander as a deliverer who was freeing them from the rule of the Persians, whom they detested. They turned over their entire treasury to him and crowned the 24-year-old Macedonian pharaoh (king) of Egypt. Along with the title came the status of a god: The Egyptians considered Alexander (and all their pharaohs) to be the son of Ammon, their most important god. This made a deep impression on the young king, who had never considered himself an ordinary mortal. He began to wear a headdress adorned with two rams' horns, a sacred symbol also depicted by the Egyptians as being worn by Ammon. Alexander spent six months in Egypt, where he founded the great ancient city of Alexandria. Alexandria grew into a worldwide center of culture and learning, and is still a thriving and respected metropolis today.

The Battle of Gaugamela

Alexander left Egypt in the spring of 331 B.C.E. and returned to Tyre to gather his troops. Through the spring and summer, they prepared for their next battle, at Gaugamela, which would turn out to be the decisive clash for the Persian Empire.

King Darius had been preparing for this encounter with Alexander since his humiliating defeat at Issus. He amassed a large number of soldiers and added new weapons to his arsenal. He fitted the wheels of 200 chariots with razor-sharp, curved blades that could slash the legs of the enemy's horses and foot soldiers. He also brought in 15 Indian war elephants.

The battle took place near the village of Gaugamela, east of the Tigris River in what is now Iraq. Darius chose the broad plain as the battle site to make sure his troops would not get hemmed in as they had at Granicus and Issus. He had workers smooth over rough spots on the field to level the ground for his special chariots. In some spots, his soldiers placed metal spikes on the ground to cripple the Macedonian horses.

Alexander reportedly had 40,000 infantry and 7,000 cavalry. Estimates of the size of Darius's army range from 250,000 to 1 million soldiers. Alexander lured the Persians into attacking his right and left flanks. This opened up a gap in their center, where Darius was fighting. Seizing the moment, Alexander quickly led his cavalry through to the center and galloped toward Darius, killing his chariot driver. Before he could get to the Persian king, however, Darius leapt from the chariot and fled the battlefield on horseback. Most of his men soon followed. Estimates of casualties at Gaugamela vary, depending on the source. Historians have estimated the Persians lost anywhere from 40,000 to 200,000 soldiers. Macedonian losses have been estimated at 150 to 1200 soldiers.

Some historians call the Battle of Gaugamela the greatest battle of antiquity. Its outcome changed the course of history, ending more than two centuries of Persian rule in Asia.

Alexander's Army

During Alexander's time, soldiers fought on foot and on horseback, meeting each other on the battlefield face to face. There were no guns, bombs, or tanks; weapons included bows and arrows, swords, spears, chariots, javelins, catapults, and special artillery used for sieges.

Alexander inherited from his father the best army of his day. When Philip became king of Macedonia in 359 B.C.E., Greek armies consisted of both civilians and professional soldiers. His first innovation was to create the world's only completely professional army. By using only professionals, warfare was no longer a seasonal activity–fought when the soldier/farmers did not have to tend their fields–but became possible year round.

All the helmets, shields, and weapons were made by skilled metalworkers, who beat the armor into shape from sheets of bronze. Iron was used for spearheads and swords because it is a much harder metal.

The infantry was the backbone of Alexander's army. More than twice as many soldiers made up the infantry as the cavalry. The infantry included mercenary soldiers from a variety of

Alexander as a God
The Egyptians considered Alexander to be the son of the god Ammon, and he began to wear a headdress adorned with rams' horns, a sacred symbol Ammon wore. This silver coin showing Alexander's image (c. 305–281 B.C.E.) comes from Thrace.

CONNECTIONS >>>>>>>>>>>>>>>>>>>>>>>>>>>>>>>>>>

Alexandria, Egypt

Among the myths that persist about Alexander the Great is that he founded 57 ancient cities. Mostly, though, what he founded were military outposts, and according to modern scholars, only six cities can be directly attributed to Alexander by either literary or archaeological evidence. We do know, though, that the ancient world through which Alexander passed ended up with many cities named Alexandria.

The first Alexandria, and one Alexander certainly founded himself, was in Egypt. Alexander located the city near the mouth of the Nile, on the Mediterranean Sea, intending it to develop into a center of commerce between Egypt and the Mediterranean. He helped plan the city, designing the streets to run in a grid pattern of straight lines.

A diverse population of Greeks, Egyptians, Persians, Syrians, and Jews soon settled in Alexandria, which remained a center of commerce, culture, and learning for the next thousand years. About 1,000 ships could use its docks at a time. Its library, built shortly after Alexander's death, was famous throughout the ancient world. It contained the world's largest collection of scrolls—about 500,000 volumes—and scholars came from all over the world to study them.

Today, Alexandria is a thriving city of about 3 million people. It is the second largest city in Egypt, and is still Egypt's chief port. Merchant ships have sailed to and from its harbors for the last 2,300 years. Historians consider the city of Alexandria to be among the most important results of Alexander's conquests.

places, including Agranians (natives of modern Bulgaria), Thracians, Cretans, and Paeonians, and was broken up into units according to nationality. Each unit had its own distinctive armor.

Infantry soldiers were called hoplites, and they generally fought in a formation called a phalanx, which was developed by the Greeks. But Philip transformed the Greek phalanx into a devastating formation, the Macedonian phalanx. In the Greek phalanx (the word is Greek and means "finger bone") soldiers were arranged in rows. The men stood in solid ranks, forming a tight rectangle. Their shields covered their own left shoulders and overlapped each other, so that each hoplite's shield also protected the man to his left. But because of their heavy shield, held in the left arm, the Greek hoplites could only use a relatively short spear in the right hand.

Philip replaced the large shield with a smaller one slung over the left shoulder. This enabled the new phalanx to carry a long lance, called a *sarissa*, in both hands. The *sarissa* was made of wood and had an iron tip. It was so long—estimates are from about 16 feet to as much as 24 feet—that even those carried by men in the back rows protruded beyond the front row of men. From the front, a phalanx resembled a giant porcupine or hedgehog: It was 16 rows deep, and the *sarissas* of the first five rows pointed forward, producing an impregnable forest of armor-piercing iron. The other rows held their *sarissas* at an angle upward, forming an effective protection against objects hurled at them. A phalanx operated much like a modern-day tank It could move in a straight, angled, or curved line, or swing around as a solid mass to face the opposite direction.

Held horizontally and thrust forward during a charge, the *sarissas* sliced through the enemy while keeping the members of the phalanx at such a distance that they could not be attacked themselves. This was a great advantage in itself. But additionally, when these awesome weapons were held upright together, they created a wall of spears, shielding from the enemy's view any maneuvers going on behind the phalanx. This was a great aid to surprise moves. Seeing the deadly wall of a phalanx's spikes coming toward them must have had a terrifying effect on Alexander's enemies.

The phalanxes were generally used to pin down the enemy's army so the cavalry could attack. The Companion cavalry was an elite body of upperclass Macedonians led in battle by Alexander himself. He adopted this innovation from his father. A highly disciplined cavalry could turn an enemy's flank, cut off its retreat, or pursue fleeing soldiers, and Philip's cavalry was just such a body. The Macedonian cavalry changed the nature of warfare, in particular because the phalanx was such a sophisticated and terrifying method of attack, later adopted by other leaders. Alexander went on to develop his father's methods further, employing them to great advantage across two continents.

Alexander's cavalry squadrons were divided into platoons. Their commanders were chosen for personal merit rather than race or birth. Armed with *sarissas* and outfitted with open-faced iron helmets and short body armor that protected their chests and backs, these troops were the most effective cavalry in the ancient world.

The cavalry used formal, strict formations, such as wedges and diamonds. The officer at the tip of the formation would find weak points in the enemy's line and then order a charge. Even though they had no stirrups and only makeshift saddles (stirrups and saddles had not yet been invented), the cavalry charged at a gallop, brandishing their *sarissas*. They were trained to respond immediately to commands on the field of

TACTICS AND STRATEGY

Warfare involves both tactics and strategy. Tactics are the techniques and procedures used by soldiers in the heat of battle, and strategy is the overall battle plan, worked out in advance. Alexander came up with brilliant strategies that were later adopted by other generals, such as Napoleon. But a good strategy only works if the enemy does exactly what they are expected to do. Since this rarely happens, it is equally important for a great general to be good at tactics—the art of maneuvering forces in combat. Alexander is also considered one of the greatest tacticians in military history. These two gifts are rarely combined in one military leader.

battle. They could drive home a charge and then immediately reform, ready for another order. The phalanx and the cavalry trained together to coordinate their actions.

Alexander's use of huge siege machines at Tyre introduced a new age of warfare. Between 332 and 326 B.C.E., the invading king mounted 15 sieges. His mechanics and engineers developed special weapons for sieges, including battering rams, catapults, and mobile towers.

Special catapults could hurl 175-pound stone blocks as far as 500 feet onto a battlefield or over a wall. They were also used to hurl large arrows and possibly even poisonous snakes and hornet nests. Ballistae were another kind of siege weapon. Similar to huge crossbows, these stable weapons shot arrows that were up to three feet long. Soldiers would often set fire to the giant arrows before launching them.

Although the Macedonian army was a much stronger fighting force than its navy, Alexander used many different kinds of ships in his cam-

Formidable Formation
The Macedonian phalanx was an innovation of Philip II. Soldiers carried small shields and long lances.

paigns. The most famous were Athenian triremes—Greek battleships that had three banks of 200 oarsmen each. They weighed up to 2,200 pounds but were swift and easy to maneuver. The oarsmen rowed in unison at a speed of up to 18 beats per minute. The beat of a gong or a drum was used to maintain this rhythm.

The main weapon of the trireme was a battering ram that protruded from the bow at water level. It was made of oak and reinforced with a bronze cap. The rowers propelled the trireme against an enemy hull. The ram pierced the hull, while the rowers back-pedaled to free their trireme from the sinking ship. Naval artillery was also an innovation of Alexander's navy. On-board weapons included large catapults and smaller swiveling catapults.

The navy sailed on seas, rivers, and small bodies of water. The triremes were swift and powerful, but because they carried so many men there was not a lot of room onboard for provisions. This meant that typically they could not stay at sea for long stretches at a time. The triremes traveled from one island to the next, or stopped frequently along the shore, and they almost always beached for the night.

How Alexander Beat Darius

Alexander was greatly outnumbered and overmatched by Darius in almost every way. The Persians had many more troops and ships and much greater wealth. With a force of Greek mercenaries estimated at up to 50,000, they may have even had more Greek soldiers fighting on their side than Alexander had on his.

Even the size of the two men made them unequal. Darius, then in his mid-40s, was said to have been nearly six and a half feet tall—huge for the time. Alexander was of medium height.

Yet Alexander had a number of advantages that enabled him to overcome his enemy's strength and stature. Alexander's troops, inherited from his father, were the most powerful fighters in the world. They were extremely disciplined and committed, even devoted, to their leader. Not until gunpowder was introduced 18 centuries later did a stronger army come along. The Persian forces were not as well trained, well disciplined, or devoted. Their size even worked against them at times, as they were not as fast or flexible as Alexander's army.

Alexander was an expert at analyzing what his available men and weapons could do, at coordinating his troops for complex battle maneuvers, and at hiding their real numbers. An incredible tactical genius, he was able to seize opportunities that opened up during a battle and organize his troops on the spot to make the most of their abilities and to exploit his enemy's weaknesses and mistakes.

One of the young king's greatest advantages was his bravery. A courageous and even reckless leader, he always led his troops into battle. His helmet was made of iron and burnished so that everyone could see him on the battlefield. Two long white plumes, called wings, rose from it, to make sure that even at great distances his men could see that he was fighting along with them.

Alexander inspired a rare depth of loyalty in his men. This was partly due to the stirring speeches he gave before battles. He also treated his soldiers very well, and knew a great number of them by name. He also had tremendous charisma, or personal magnetism and charm. (The English form of this word is based on the Greek word *kharisma*, which means "divine favor.") Many of Alexander's men believed that the gods favored their ruler and his cause. Because of this, they were willing to follow him into battles and fight bravely, even when they were outnumbered.

Another factor is that the Persians underestimated Alexander, especially in the beginning. In fact, Memnon (380–333 B.C.E.), the general leading the Greek mercenaries that fought for the Persians, came up with a plan early on that most likely would have defeated Alexander. Before the battle of Granicus, Memnon suggested that instead of fighting the Macedonians, the Persians starve them out by burning the cities and destroying the crops in their path. He knew that the Macedonian army, no matter how fierce, would not be able to survive for long without food and supplies. But Darius's commanders rejected Memnon's plan because they were sure they could crush this small invading force, led by an inexperienced young man. Had they listened to their Greek employee, who understood better what they were up against, Alexander's name might have been Alexander the Obscure instead of Alexander the Great.

Divide and Conquer

A medieval military drawing illustrates how Alexander's cavalry could be used to drive a wedge into an enemy's army.

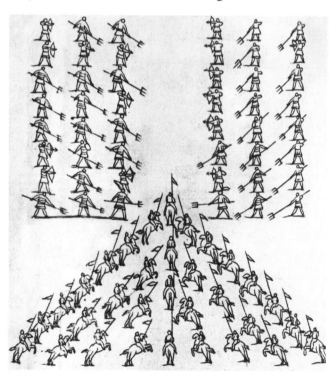

Alexander's Weapons

Catapult: The Greeks invented catapults in about 400 B.C.E. Philip was the first commander to use siege weapons on the battlefield, and Alexander adopted the same practice. His soldiers used smaller, mobile catapults to fire large arrows aimed at individual soldiers and stones, or bags of stones, capable of killing or wounding a number of men with a single shot.

Catapults were still in use in the 20th century. In World War I, soldiers in trenches made catapults by hand. They would use them to propel grenades and poison gas canisters at the enemy. Since World War II, catapults have been used to launch jets from aircraft carriers. During that war catapults were hydraulic, but later the British invented a steam-powered catapult. Commonly used today, the steam-powered catapult launches a jet fighter at full throttle, giving it the power to accelerate from zero to 165 miles in two seconds—enough to get it airborne from the relatively short distance of the aircraft carrier's deck. In the 21st century experimentation is in progress with even more sophisticated and powerful catapults.

Battering Ram: The battering rams used by ancient armies were most often made of the largest tree trunk possible, which had been hacked to a point at one end. The tree trunk would then be set on wheels, or sometimes carried by men, and rammed through the doors and walls of fortresses and castles.

Sometimes a battering ram was slung in a support frame so that it could be repeatedly swung against the barricade.

Modern battering rams are usually used by police forces, most often by special paramilitary units known as SWAT (special weapons and tactics) teams, which are specially trained for dangerous missions. Sometimes these battering rams are attached to cars or other heavy vehicles and sometimes they are smaller, operated by just two or three officers to break down a door.

Ballistae: Ballistae were giant crossbows powerful enough to shoot huge darts or arrows, singly or in bunches. Ballistae were generally designed on a horizontal plane with arms of wood. Human hair or animal sinew was wrapped around each arm and acted like a spring to send the darts or arrows hurtling forward. Ballistae were extremely accurate in hitting intended targets but had the disadvantage of not being able to travel very far.

The Greek word *ballista* originates from another Greek word, *ballei*, meaning "to throw." These words are also the ancient roots of our modern word *ballistics,* the science of the way projectiles move in flight, or more specifically, the study of what happens when firearms are fired. Most people today have heard of ballistic missiles. These are one of the more destructive modern equivalents of ancient projectile weaponry.

CHAPTER 2

The Empire at Its Largest

HIS VICTORY AT THE BATTLE OF GAUGAMELA ESTABLISHED Alexander the Great as the ruler of the Persian Empire. Only three years after he first invaded Asia Minor, he was hailed as the new Great King of Persia and Lord of Asia–the ruler of all Persian lands.

But as long as Darius III was alive, he remained a threat to Alexander's rule. As soon as Alexander was able to break away from the fighting at Gaugamela, he began his pursuit of Darius. Alexander pursued the older king through the night, but Darius escaped into the mountains. Alexander decided to wait, rather than to push through dangerous mountain passes where troops still loyal to Darius could ambush the Macedonians.

Darius had abandoned some of his treasure near Gaugamela, and Alexander used the loot to reward his soldiers. He then traveled south along the Royal Road, built centuries before, to Babylon (located near what is now Baghdad). He expected opposition, but instead, because the Persian king was so unpopular, the Babylonians welcomed the soldiers with trumpets and showered them with flowers. The young king's popularity grew when he promised to rebuild the temple to the chief Babylonian god, Bel Marduk, which the Persians had destroyed.

The Macedonians and Greeks were amazed by the wealth and majesty of Babylon. This fabled city already had a history dating back to about 2000 B.C.E. Nearly five times larger than Athens, it was organized around a seven-story tower–which may have been the famous Tower of Babel.

During the five weeks the Macedonian troops remained there, Alexander took up residence in one of Babylon's two royal palaces. The palace had about 600 rooms and its terraces of trees, flowers, and shrubs,

OPPOSITE
Lost Wonder
Little of the great palace at Persepolis (in modern Iran) remained after the Macedonians set it on fire. This stairway dates from the sixth to fifth century B.C.E.

The Tower of Babel

The Tower of Babel (Babel and Babylon come from the same Hebrew word, *babel* or *bavel*, meaning "gate of God") is the subject of a story in the Old Testament of the Bible. According to this story, found in Genesis 11:1-9, the people of Babel built the tower in order to climb to heaven. Angered at their idea that they could reach heaven without God's help, God punished the builders by causing them to speak different languages. Being unable to communicate with each other, they were unable to complete the tower.

Many scholars believe this story may be an attempt by the ancient Hebrews to explain how different languages came into being. Some biblical scholars believe the story is a metaphor about ambition. However, it is likely that the so-called Tower of Babel itself did exist in ancient Babylon, as an actual tower, or ziggurat, built for use as a temple.

The Babylonian ziggurats were traditionally built in the shapes of pyramids, with each layer smaller than the one below it. Often these terraced towers were built to honor particular gods, and some cities had several ziggurats. The top story, which was used both as a temple and as an astronomical observatory, often contained a sanctuary.

Historians dispute the date the Tower of Babel was built. It may have been around 2200 B.C.E. It is believed that King Nebuchadnezzar II (605–562 B.C.E.) later rebuilt the Tower of Babel to a height of about 300 feet.

Archaeologists have found the ruins of several Babylonian ziggurats. They are not certain which of these, if any, is the Tower of Babel referred to in the Bible. Many believe it is the seven-story tower of Etemenaki, built to honor the Babylonian god Marduk, and whose ruins lie near the Euphrates River.

called the Hanging Gardens, were known far and wide. Among the Persian treasures was a large quantity of bullion (bars of silver and gold). Alexander is said to have used some of it to give the soldiers nearly a whole year's extra pay.

Alexander began a practice of appointing local Persian officials to leading positions. In Babylon, he allowed the local satrap to remain in that position. Although his soldiers resented this, it was a wise policy. It meant that uprisings would be less likely, and other Persian satraps would be more willing to surrender if they knew they were likely to be reappointed. Alexander also separated the civil government from the military. Leaving a military force under Macedonian command in Babylon, he pushed farther east.

Susa and Persepolis

In November 331 B.C.E., Alexander set out for the administrative center of the Persian Empire, Susa, a spot that today is about 30 miles from the city of Shustar in Iran. On the way, he met up with about 15,000 reinforcements from Greece whom he had summoned nearly a year before. Their arrival increased his military strength significantly. When the troops arrived in Susa in December, the city surrendered and turned over its treasury.

Alexander's soldiers were once again astonished by the wealth of the Persians. They discovered more gold and silver, much of it looted from Greece by the Persians more than 100 years before. They also found furnishings, tapestries, and jewels. There were piles of purple embroidery that had remained fresh for nearly 200 years because of the honey and olive oil that had been mixed into their dyes. Alexander handed out more gifts to his men and sent a small part of the Susa treasure to Athens. That small portion, however, was equal to six times Athens's yearly income at the time.

Susa was the home of Darius's mother, Sisygambis, his daughters, and members of his harem, all of whom had been traveling under the protection of Alexander's army. Now Alexander installed them in their palace at Susa.

CONNECTIONS >>>>>>>>>>>>

Babylon Revisited

The awe-inspiring ancient city of Babylon, which lay on the Euphrates River in what is now Iraq, was the largest and most sophisticated city in the world when Alexander arrived there. The crown jewel of that city was its huge and elaborate system of palaces, built by the tyrant King Nebuchadnezzar II.

In 1978, Iraq's modern-day ruler, Saddam Hussein (b. 1937), ordered archaeologists to unearth and restore the remains of Nebuchadnezzar's lost city and its palaces. Just as Nebuchadnezzar had done, Hussein had each of approximately 6 million bricks used to build the palace inscribed with his own name. When archaeologists discovered that the ancient city gate was adorned with a plaque proclaiming the glory of Nebuchadnezzar, Hussein was not to be outdone. He ordered a matching plaque honoring himself and demanded it be mounted on the opposite side of the gate from the Nebuchadnezzar plaque.

After nine years of ongoing restoration, Hussein was ready to celebrate his link with the former ruler of Babylon. In 1987, he held the First International Babylon Festival, for which he had a special seal created. The commemorative seal showed himself and Nebuchadnezzar side by side and Hussein reportedly enjoyed pointing out their physical similarity.

In a story that suggests modern history does sometimes echo the past, the book of Daniel in the Bible tells us that before repenting of his sins before God, Nebuchadnezzar ". . . was driven from men; and did eat grass as oxen, and . . . his hair was grown like eagles' [feathers], and his nails like birds' [claws]." (*King James Bible, Book of Daniel* 4:33)

The King is Conquered
This painting shows Darius in his battle dress, at war with Alexander. It was done on the wall of the home of Cassander of Macedon, who lived in ancient Pompeii.

While in the city, Alexander also reorganized his army to prepare for warfare in the wilder, more mountainous country where they would hunt for Darius. He divided the troops into smaller units of 75 to 100 men and appointed many new officers. Up until that time, the Macedonian military units were organized according to the provinces of their kingdom. For the first time, Alexander selected officers based on merit—an indication that he wanted to do away with regional divisions. The army also changed its method of sending signals from bugle calls to the Persian method of using a bonfire to send smoke signals.

Alexander appointed the Persian commander of Susa's garrison as satrap of the region. In December 331 B.C.E., he and his troops once again took to the road. As usual, they left soldiers behind, led by a Macedonian. With a refreshed army of an estimated 60,000, Alexander marched toward the city of Persepolis, the ceremonial center of the Persian Empire and the winter home of the Persian kings. On the way, the army met resistance in a narrow mountain pass known as the Persian Gates. The challengers were probably the last holdouts of Darius's army. Alexander divided his army into two branches to get through.

Arriving successfully in Persepolis, the Macedonians found the largest treasure of all. A vast storehouse of gold and silver, it was said to be the largest single fortune in the world. The treasure was so enormous that it took more than 500 camels and more than 4,000 mules to transport it back to Macedonia. The treasure weighed around 7,300 tons, and was enough for Alexander to pay his army for 25 years.

Night of Destruction

On April 25, 330 B.C.E., the Macedonians, after a long night of drinking, burned down the great palace in Persepolis. This event has remained controversial, with different historians offering different interpretations. Many have criticized the act as barbaric, not to mention unwise, since the Macedonians now controlled the city. Other historians believe that destroying the palace was an act of vengeance. Built by King Darius I (d. c. 485 B.C.E.) in about 520 B.C.E., the magnificent structure had later been the home of King Xerxes I (519–465 B.C.E.), who had destroyed many Greek temples when he invaded Greece in 480 B.C.E. Still other historians claim that Persepolis was a symbol of the rule of Darius III. They suggest that destroying it was a dramatic way for Alexander to demonstrate the end of the Persian Empire. (Ironically, destroying the palace may have been the best thing that could have happened to it. It became the era's best preserved ruins because of its long disappearance under the desert sands.)

It was probably not an easy decision. On one hand, as a Macedonian, Alexander identified deeply with Greek culture. He had come to Persia partly to avenge the wrongs Persia had committed against Greece. But he was also warming to his role as Persia's exalted ruler. He admired and

CONNECTIONS >>>>>>>>>>>>>>>>>>>>>>>>>>>>>>>>

Persepolis

In the language of the Persians, the name of their magnificent city was Takht-e-Jamshid. Meaning "the throne of Jamshid," the name honored a mythical Persian king. In the West we know it by its Greek name, Persepolis. From about 500 B.C.E., the capital city of the Persian Empire was called Persa. Add *Persa* to the Greek word for city, *polis*, and it is easy to see how the Greeks derived their version of the name—Persepolis, or City of Persians.

Technically speaking, Persepolis was not really a city at all. It was a series of palaces and treasuries that formed a ceremonial center, attended by a small town of guards and caretakers. Each year at the Persian New Year's festival, envoys from all the nations subject to the Persians arrived at Persepolis to renew their loyalty to the king, bringing lavish gifts. The treasures were deposited at Persepolis, where they accumulated over many decades.

Although Alexander destroyed the great palace complex of Persepolis, it has not been entirely lost to us. Since the early 20th century, archaeologists have excavated many of its huge structures. One of the most stunning of these is the palace's *apadana*, or reception hall, where in ancient times the great Persian kings received tribute from subjects who came from far and wide. Today, the *apadana* is marked only by a wide field of pillars adorned with elaborately carved horse heads—a surrealistic site in the midst of a bare red desert in southwest Iran. UNESCO declared the city of Persepolis a World Heritage Site in 1979.

appreciated many things about this ancient civilization. He wanted to be accepted by the Persian ruling class. He began to adopt Persian ways and brought Persian attendants into his inner circles. Forced to share power with the Persians, some of the Macedonian soldiers began to feel discontented.

While in Persepolis, Alexander discovered that Darius had fled to his summer palace in Ecbatana (now the city of Hamadân in modern Iran). He was traveling with what was left of his army, whose numbers had been greatly reduced because so many soldiers had defected or been killed. The remaining troops numbered only about 9,000 men, including Greek mercenaries. In the spring of 329 B.C.E., Alexander and some of his troops pushed north through the mountains toward the Caspian Sea in pursuit of Darius.

The Betrayal of Darius

Hearing a report of Alexander's approach, Darius and his men began riding east. Several of his own officers took the Persian king prisoner and threw him into a wagon, believing he was too weak a leader to be left in control. Alexander set out after them with about 500 men, leaving his second-in-command, General Parmenion (400–330 B.C.E.), in charge at Ec-

The Hindu Kush
The Hindu Kush Mountains look as forbidding today as they did in Alexander's time. This track leading to the mountains is in Badakhshan, Afghanistan.

batana. They traveled across the desert, covering more than 440 miles in just 11 days. After the long, exhausting chase, they came upon Darius's camp at dawn. But Alexander did not get the chance to take his revenge. Bessus (d. 329 B.C.E.), the leader of the revolt against Darius and the satrap of a region called Bactria, stabbed Darius to death just before Alexander's arrival. Alexander covered Darius's body with his cloak. He sent his former enemy's body back to Persepolis, ordering that a royal funeral be held.

One of Bessus's accomplices, Nabarzanes (dates unknown), surrendered to Alexander and was pardoned. He also released those mercenaries who had joined the Persians before Greece and Macedonia declared war on them. The others were required to serve in Alexander's army for the same pay that Darius had given them. Obviously, Alexander's view of mercenaries had changed since the Battle of Granicus, when Greek soldiers fighting for the Persians had been murdered or enslaved as traitors.

Alexander then turned his attention to the pursuit of a new target: Bessus. The satrap had proclaimed himself Darius's successor and was fleeing to his home region of Bactria, in what is now Afghanistan. Alexander spent much of the next year hunting him. Bactria was at the eastern edge of a wilderness of vast deserts and rugged mountains. After their conquests of the three royal cities, Alexander and his men headed east from Persepolis into this sterile terrain—a region populated by fierce nomadic tribes. To conquer the east, they would not only have to do battle with this new kind of opponent, but with the elements as well. Thirst, hunger, heat, and cold were to become the soldiers' new enemies during the long marches ahead.

Murder Plot

In October 330 B.C.E., Alexander learned of a plot against his life. The accused man, Philotas (d. 330 B.C.E.), was a lifelong friend of Alexander's and the commander of the Companion cavalry. He was also the son of Alexander's second in command, Parmenion. Philotas himself was not the plotter, but was said to have heard about a conspiracy against Alexander and failed to report it. The Macedonian army found him guilty of treason. He and several others were executed.

Alexander then sent soldiers to Ecbatana where Parmenion was stationed. He, too, was executed. It

Alexander the Invincible

During his Asian campaigns, Alexander was injured at least 10 times. He was wounded by nearly every kind of weapon, including swords, clubs, daggers, stones, and arrows. In the battle against the Mallians, when an arrow pierced the king's lung, his troops thought their leader had been killed. They were so enraged that they ran through the city killing everyone they could find. Alexander made it through with a splintered rib and a torn lung.

During the siege of Gaza, he was badly wounded in the shoulder and lost a great deal of blood when he was hit by a catapult bolt.

While invading Samarqand, an arrow split a bone in his leg, making it impossible for him to ride his horse. At first, the infantry got the honor of carrying Alexander, but soon the cavalry became jealous of their privilege and demanded to dismount so they could carry him. Alexander decided to let each unit take turns sharing the honor.

Alexander also lived through various other minor and serious wounds and illnesses. These ranged from a bird dropping a stone on his head to getting a mild case of hypothermia while crossing the Cydnus (now called the Tarsus) River.

is unclear whether he was guilty of anything, but even if he was innocent, the tradition of the Macedonian blood-feud would have required the soldiers to kill him. Otherwise he might have felt bound to avenge his son's death. The deaths of Philotas and Parmenion added to the poor morale among the troops, which had begun with Alexander's appointment of Persians to high positions.

Many of the men felt the war was over and wanted to go home, rather than pursue Bessus in the east. But Alexander was determined to conquer the eastern half of the empire and knew that Bessus was a bold, skillful warrior who was popular enough to organize a resistance. Moreover, Bessus was well-acquainted with the back hills and the tribes who lived in them, and would be fighting on familiar terrain. Alexander, driven by his desire to conquer, felt compelled to stop him. But Alexander's personal drive and courage were not enough—he needed his army behind him. Now they stood at the threshold of a mutiny. In a rousing speech, he offered lavish gifts to any soldiers who continued on with him. He heightened his troops' motivation by declaring that they stood on the threshold of victory. He assured them that Bessus was nothing more than a barbarian chieftain and would be easy to defeat. There was no mutiny.

Death Marches

As Alexander and his troops pursued Bessus into Bactria, the young king found himself confronted with an extremely important strategic decision. The most direct way to Bactria was a route through the Kara Kum Desert that was part of the long trade route that later came to be known as the Silk Road. The other road detoured south through several towns and then across the Hindu Kush, one of the major mountain ranges in central Asia. (Today, the Hindu Kush mountains separate Kabul in Afghanistan from central Asia.) The first route was easier and shorter, but it exposed Alexander and his men to attack from Bessus's dangerous mounted archers. Alexander chose the southern route, taking a wide loop before heading north again up into what is now Kabul and Begram. In late May of 329 B.C.E., he marched with his troops into the Hindu Kush mountains. His teacher, Aristotle, believed that from their summit, one would be able to see the end of the world.

Crossing the Hindu Kush is considered by many historians to be an achievement unparalleled in world history—and one of the most incredible accomplishments of Alexander's career. It required extreme levels of endurance and extraordinary leadership. The highest peak of the Hindu Kush

A Dying Culture

The Khawak Pass and the route Alexander took through the Hindu Kush are today nearly as difficult to navigate as they were in the fourth century B.C.E. The Chitral a region of the Hindu Kush in what is today Pakistan, is one of the most remote and inaccessible parts of the world, but the Macedonian army made its way through.

In the deep mountain valleys above Chitral they encountered the Kalash tribes, the so-called black pagans (named as such by later conquering Arabs, who were unable to convert the Kalash to Islam and still have not today). The Kalash dressed in black robes, ornamented themselves with intricately woven cowrie shell headdresses, and, according to their religious custom, placed their dead in open coffins and left them out for wild animals to consume.

Today, much of this cultural tradition remains. The coarse black clothing, the cowrie shells, the carved wooden coffins, and ritual religious dancing have not been entirely lost. A regional legend still insists that the current Kalash people are descended from the unions between the area's ancient native people and Macedonian soldiers who passed through with Alexander—many of whom, it is said, stayed or returned later to establish homes there themselves.

To historians and archaeologists this idea is not all that far-fetched. There are still strong hints of some kind of Indo-European cultural mix, including the knowledge of wine-making and the fact that many of the Kalash still worship the sky god, Di Zau, said to be the brother of Greece's mightiest god, Zeus.

Today's remaining Kalash, estimated at about 3,000 people, are perhaps the last surviving ancestors of those who lived in the area when Alexander's troops marched through. But their ancient culture is now threatened with extinction as unchecked tourism makes drastic inroads into their way of life. With encouragement from the Pakistani government, tour providers heavily promote the Kalash mountain valleys to those who seek exotic, out-of-the-way adventures that feature "quaint" regional peoples and "never before seen" customs and culture.

The local outcry against these efforts, which include the building of modern tourist hotels, some on sacred Kalash sites, and logging of the people's lands to the point of deforestation, is fierce. But the cry is hard to hear in a world where modern life is like a roaring beast quick to devour anything "old-fashioned." This once hidden and nearly untouchable corner of the globe may not remain a secret much longer.

More can be learned about the Kalash from the Indigenous Peoples Survival Foundation (IPSF), a humanitarian organization, at www.indigenouspeople.org.

is more than 25,000 feet above sea level, making it one of the highest mountains in the world. The army crossed over the 12,000-foot Khawak Pass. They were forced to travel single file along narrow paths, which stretched the troops out over miles.

Many of the men got altitude sickness. The intense glare caused snow blindness. There was a shortage of provisions, and nothing grew in the area except herbs. Supplies could not be moved by wagon, and the pack animals that carried them frequently fell on the dangerous, snow-covered roads. The men ate the dead mules raw because there was no cooking fuel. Men died of cold, hunger, and thirst.

Alexander may have lost more than 2,000 men in the march across the Hindu Kush. He arrived in Bactria with fewer than 32,000 soldiers. He released the older and sick ones from service and set off with the remaining troops, chasing Bessus toward the Oxus River.

Fierce Warrior

A detail from a first century B.C.E. Roman mosaic shows Alexander the Great at the Battle of Issus.

Down out of the mountains, the soldiers faced another ordeal: heat. They had to march at night across 46.6 miles of waterless desert, because it was too hot to travel during the day. The shifting sands made travel especially difficult. The men used up all their water. A famous story about this march is that when one of the men found a small pool of water, he offered it first to Alexander. The king refused it, saying that he would drink only when all his soldiers had had water. It was this kind of behavior that inspired such fierce loyalty.

When the army finally reached the river, many soldiers, including Alexander, drank too much water and became ill. Many of them died.

Meanwhile, Bessus fled through Bactria. His troops, from Bactria and Sogdiana, were on familiar terrain. (The satrapies of Bactria and Sogdiana were located in more or less the same areas as modern Afghanistan, Uzbekistan, and western Tajikistan.) They burned the earth behind them as they fled, so that their pursuers would find no food. After they crossed the Oxus, they burned all the available ships to prevent Alexander's men from crossing the river. The Macedonians, however, made rafts by stuffing animal skins and tents with hay. Five days later, the army reached the opposite bank.

Crossing the Hindu Kush, the desert, and the Oxus River made Alexander's army seem unstoppable. In June of 329 B.C.E., about a year after Alexander began chasing him, one of Bessus's allies, the Sogdian leader Spitamenes, arrested him. Bessus was brought naked in bonds to the town of Bactra. Alexander turned him over to the Persian people, who tried him for killing their king. He was found guilty and executed.

Guerrilla Warfare

Since they had left the three Persian capitals, Alexander and his men had been fighting a different kind of war. The mountainous region to the east of the three royal cities was made up of independent, fierce tribes and bandits. These people were unknown to the Greeks, and the Persians had only barely managed to dominate them. Even the Persian kings had to pay tribute before the tribes would allow them to pass through their lands.

The Sogdians and the other tribes who joined forces with them to fight Alexander were excellent mounted archers. Instead of pitched battles fought by armies facing one another on a battlefield, this new phase of the campaign involved guerrilla warfare. The Bactrians and the Sogdians, who lived in what is now Turkestan, did not fight in the traditional Greek/Macedonian style. Much of the landscape was dusty steppe country—semi-arid grass-covered plains—that was unsuited for phalanx maneuvers.

In response, Alexander reorganized his cavalry, creating new formations that were better suited for the new terrain. He also brought native horsemen into the army. Alexander's ability to successfully adapt his strategy and tactics to many different kinds of warfare, including major battles, sieges, skirmishes, and guerrilla opposition, sets him apart from other great commanders who were skilled primarily in conventional, open warfare.

The Macedonian army proceeded from its base in Maracanda, near modern-day Samarqand, to the Jaxartes River. They considered this the end of Asia. In July 329 B.C.E., Alexander founded a new city, called Alexandria Eschate, which means "the farthest Alexandria," on the northeast border of the Persian Empire (the modern city of Khodzent in Tajikistan).

A BELOVED HORSE

As a boy, Alexander succeeded in taming a wild horse owned by his father that no one else had been able to even get near. The young prince named the horse Bucephalas (which means "ox head" because he had a natural mark on his coat that was shaped like the head of an ox) and rode him from then on. Years later, while Alexander was battling in the East, bandits snuck into the Macedonians' camp one night and made off with some of their horses. Among them was Alexander's beloved warhorse. He sent word out to the tribes that Bucephalas must be returned or he would devastate the entire countryside. The thieves returned the now aging horse, for which Alexander rewarded them.

Messengers arrived, telling the Macedonians that the tribes of Sogdiana had risen up in revolt behind them. Their leader was a warlord named Spitamenes (370–328 B.C.E.), the same man who had turned Bessus over to Alexander.

Spitamenes may have been the one enemy Alexander ever underestimated. Though he possessed a smaller army than Alexander's, Spitamenes was probably the most determined opponent he encountered in his campaigns. It would take Alexander until the autumn of 328 B.C.E., more than a year, to defeat him.

Alexander spent the winter in Bactria waiting for reinforcements. His situation was precarious. Since crossing the Hindu Kush, the army had dwindled to about 30,000 men. It was never smaller than in the last months of 329 B.C.E. A total of 12,000 infantry with 2,000 cavalry eventually arrived. But the reinforcements were mostly Greek mercenaries, not Macedonians. These forces managed to capture seven Sogdian forts. During this campaign, Spitamenes's horsemen besieged the Macedonian garrison at Maracanda. When the Macedonians started to march south, the tribes attacked their rear. Alexander returned to the north and sent his Greek mercenaries to Maracanda. This turned out to be one of his few serious mistakes; Spitamenes annihilated the mercenaries. Alexander and some members of his cavalry raced to Maracanda, covering 180 miles through desert country in three days, but Spitamenes had escaped. The local population who had rebelled suffered the same fate the Tyrians had suffered: The men were killed and the women were sold as slaves.

Another of the local tribes to rebel in 328 B.C.E. were the Scythians, an extremely fierce people. Alexander was wounded in the neck during the battle to subdue them, but continued to lead his forces, which used catapults on the battlefield to defeat the Scythians. It was a turning point in the region, because many tribes were convinced that if the Scythians could not defeat Alexander, no one could. They surrendered.

Spitamenes finally came to his end in December 328 B.C.E. Deserted by his allies, he was killed by a Macedonian officer. He himself had killed about 2,000 Macedonian foot soldiers and 300 cavalry in Sogdiana.

Capturing the Sogdian Rock

In the spring of 327 B.C.E., Alexander captured one of the most secure strongholds in Asia, the Sogdian Rock, a short distance south of Maracanda. Sheer, steep cliffs protected the Sogdians, who occupied an area near the top. Their stronghold was honeycombed caves that could hold a

Rage and Murder

In Sogdiana, just before the death of Spitamenes, Alexander lost his temper in a drunken quarrel and killed a close friend, Cleitus the Black (d. 328 B.C.E.). Cleitus was the brother of Alexander's childhood nurse and one of the two commanders of the Companion cavalry. He had fought under Philip and had known Alexander his entire life. He had even saved Alexander's life at the Battle of Granicus.

There was a banquet just before Cleitus was to leave for Bactria, where he had been appointed governor. It was the Macedonian feast-day for Dionysus, the god of wine and, as was usual with Alexander and his court, the drink was flowing freely. Cleitus, becoming annoyed with Alexander's boastful, drunken ravings, made some caustic remarks. Among other complaints, he was offended by the fact that the Macedonians now had to ask Persian attendants for an audience with their king. He also objected to Persians getting positions of command.

His complaints enraged Alexander and several officers had to physically restrain their king from attacking Cleitus. There are various accounts of what happened next, but in at least one account Cleitus was hastily ushered out. He was soon back, though, with a final insult. In a rage, this story goes, Alexander grabbed a spear and murdered Cleitus with a single thrust. All stories agree that Cleitus fell dead and Alexander was left covered in his blood. Immediately overcome by remorse, reports say, the king attempted to use the same spear on himself before officers and friends prevented him from doing so.

In the following days, self-pitying and grief-stricken over his friend's death, and furious with himself about his lack of self-control, Alexander spiraled into depression. He isolated himself in his tent and refused all food, drink, or comfort. It was not until soothsayers in Alexander's entourage gave the troops justifications for the king's violent action that Alexander finally resurfaced. They claimed that the god Dionysus had possessed the king with madness to punish him for a slight on his feast day. When he recovered, Alexander made a sacrifice to appease Dionysus.

Many historians consider this one of the most tragic events in Alexander's personal history. After Cleitus's death, the army convicted the king's old friend of treason. But it was a political move, and morale sank even further.

In Cleitus's stead, Alexander appointed a Persian officer named Artabazus (389–325 B.C.E.) as satrap of Bactria. He had known Artabazus in Macedonia, where the Persian had spent many years in Philip's court during Alexander's childhood. Artabazus was also the father of a woman named Barsine (c. 363– c. 309), a childhood friend of Alexander's who became his mistress in Persia. Artabazus, who spoke both Greek and Persian, became one of Alexander's most influential Persian advisors. He suppressed a native uprising and helped convince the Persian elite to accept Alexander.

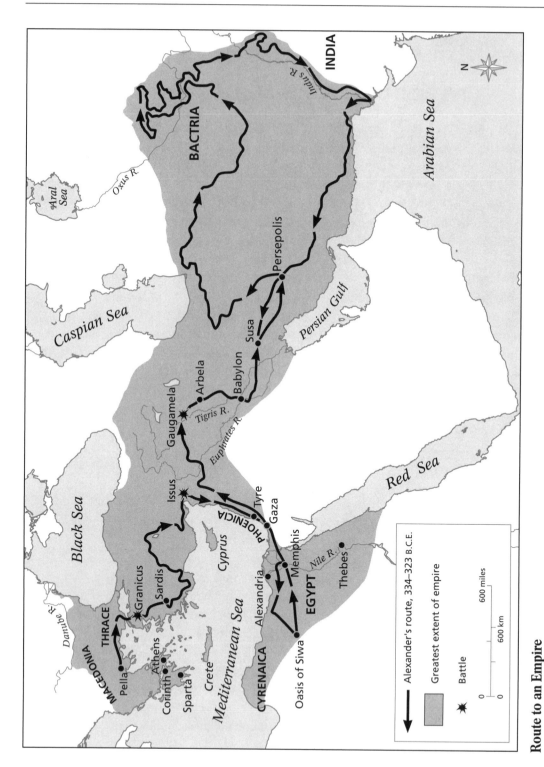

Route to an Empire

From his home base in Macedonia to the west, Alexander and his army stormed through what is know Turkey, south into Egypt, and east toward India. The arrow shows the path of his travels

small army. They had enough provisions to last for years. Their leader, Oxyartes (b. 377 B.C.E.), taunted Alexander, defying him to send up men with wings to capture the fortress.

Alexander marched his men to the base of the rock, but there was clearly no way to scale it. A single goat track led up to the Sogdian camp, which was defended by the expert Sogdian archers. The Macedonian army made camp out of the range of their arrows.

If Alexander did not conquer the Sogdians, their continued presence would always be a threat to his rule. He assembled 300 men, his best mountaineers, and offered them lavish rewards if they successfully reached the top. In the first truly dangerous mission not led by Alexander himself, the men began their climb. They chose to ascend the steepest side of the rock so they would not be seen from the caves, but about 30 of the climbers—one in 10—fell to their deaths. When the remaining men reached the top, they waved the long strips of linen they had brought with them to signal their success.

The mountaineers were unarmed because they had not been able to carry their heavy arms up on the dangerous climb. Oxyartes, however, was unaware of this. He saw only that some of Alexander's men had succeeded in reaching the top of the rock, but had no idea how many nor what weapons they had. He surrendered.

Ultimately, Alexander and Oxyartes became allies. Alexander married his daughter Roxane (343–310 B.C.E.) and their marriage helped bring about peace in Bactria and Sogdiana. Roxane gave birth to a son named Alexander (323–310 B.C.E.)—known later to historians as Alexander IV. Alexander the Great died before his son was born, and that son only lived to the age of 13. He was murdered in Macedonia along with his mother.

In the summer of 327 B.C.E., Alexander returned to Bactria, where he reinforced his troops. He ordered that 30,000 young Persians be formed into an army unit, and also added native cavalry units, including the mounted archers of the Dahae tribe. The addition of so many native soldiers to the army caused great tension among the Macedonian troops. About two-thirds of the army was ordered to stay to defend Bactria. The rest were sent north to build towns that would serve as garrisons and centers of administration. Hoping to create peace in the region, Alexander encouraged the tribal people to settle in the new towns.

By the spring of 327 B.C.E., Alexander's domain extended along and beyond the southern shores of the Caspian Sea, including modern Afghanistan and Baluchistan, and northward into Bactria and Sogdiana. It

FROM GREECE TO INDIA

At its largest, by 327 B.C.E., Alexander the Great's empire was 2 million square miles. It stretched from Greece all the way to India.

To Bow or Not to Bow

Callisthenes and other soldiers were especially critical of Alexander's attempt to introduce the practice of *proskynesis*, the eastern custom of ritual bowing to the floor before the Great King. For the Persians, bowing to the king was an expression of respect for his royal office. But for the Greeks and Macedonians, bowing was strictly reserved for the gods. They looked upon their king as a fellow warrior, not a god, and had enjoyed an open and equal relationship with Alexander. They detested the idea of bowing down to him now.

Historians have different ideas about why Alexander wanted the soldiers to practice *proskynesis*. Some see it as a sign of his increasing arrogance. He may even have begun to believe himself truly a god. Others believe that he did not want to alienate the Persians, who might have resented bowing to him when the Macedonians would not. The Persians, whose king was traditionally so exalted, may have perceived the friendly familiarity of the Macedonians as an indication that the king was not very powerful. All agree that it was difficult for Alexander to be a king to both the Persians and the Macedonians, whose traditions were so different.

One night in the summer of 327 B.C..E., at a banquet in Bactria, Alexander's closest friends convinced the other soldiers to perform *proskynesis*. Only Callisthenes refused to bow. Like Aristotle, he believed strongly in the superiority of Greek culture and later accused Alexander of wanting to be worshiped as a god. Callisthenes's death did not end his influence. Many important people in Athens were angered about his arrest and subsequent death (although it is not clear how he died), and after Alexander's death they wrote hostile and inaccurate accounts about him and joined forces with his enemies in Macedonia.

had taken him only three years, from the spring of 330 B.C.E. to the spring of 327 B.C.E., to take control of this vast area. Alexander's empire was now at its largest. Despite his desire and efforts to push on to even greater conquests, there were to be none—aside from a small bit of territory he took over in India shortly thereafter.

Another Murder

In the autumn of 327 B.C.E., another murder plot against the new ruler of the Persian Empire was revealed. The would-be assassins were six of his squires, or personal attendants. A total of about 50 young men served as Alexander's squires, and among their duties was guarding the king while he slept. According to some accounts, on the night of the planned assassination, Alexander stayed up all night drinking and talking with friends. When he found the squires waiting up for him the next morning, he praised what he assumed was their loyalty. Feeling guilty, one of the squires confessed to the murder plot. The Macedonian army found the squires guilty of treason and they were stoned to death.

Some accounts say the squires claimed that Callisthenes, the great-nephew of Alexander's teacher Aristotle, had encouraged their plot. As Alexander's official historian, Callisthenes traveled with the army, compiling an account of events as they occurred. His job was to ensure that, by keeping a written record of Alexander's exploits, widespread fame would be ensured for the great conqueror. Callisthenes also taught some of Alexander's soldiers, including the six squires. Unfortunately, only a few original fragments of his work survive, and most of what we know comes from the writings of others who read Callisthenes and other ancient historians. Callisthenes's writings served his own arrogance. He claimed that Alexander would not win glory as a result of his actions, but, rather, from the history of them that Callisthenes would write. Many of his accounts included ridiculous claims. For example, he wrote that the waves bowed down and worshiped Alexander as he passed the coast. But at the same time that he was writing these exaggerated accounts of his king's deeds for public consumption, he was criticizing Alexander in private. Like others, he was critical of Alexander's policy of appointing Persians to high positions, and his adoption of Persian customs and dress.

It is unclear exactly what became of Callisthenes after the squires' murder plot was uncovered. He was arrested and some historians believe he was then put to death. Others believe that because he was Greek, the Macedonians could not legally try him. They think he was imprisoned and died of a disease some months after his arrest.

To the Ends of the Earth

By the end of 327 B.C.E., many of Alexander's soldiers were beginning to turn against him. The deaths of Philotas and Parmenion, the appointment of Persians to high offices, the issue of *proskynesis*, Alexander's marriage to a Bactrian princess, and the arrest of Callisthenes had all contributed to the general dissatisfaction. Many soldiers assumed the expedition was over and the war won. They were ready to go home.

But Alexander had other plans. Although his original aim had been to conquer the Persian Empire, he was as much an explorer as a conqueror. Aristotle's lessons about an Encircling Ocean that the Greeks believed surrounding all the lands on Earth continued to lure Alexander. He desperately wanted to travel to the ends of the earth and stand on the banks of this ocean, and believed that the best way to reach it was through India. Relentlessly, he pushed his exhausted troops to continue marching east.

CHAPTER 3

Final Years of the Empire

BY THE SUMMER OF 327 B.C.E., ALEXANDER HAD CONQUERED nearly all of the Persian Empire. But instead of focusing on governing his vast domain, he wanted to continue traveling east–to India. He thought that when he reached its eastern edge, he would arrive at the Encircling Ocean (see page 47).

The historian Arrian (c. 86–160 B.C.E.) claimed that Alexander was motivated by pothos, a Greek word that means insatiable ambition, curiosity, or deep longing for something. Other historians think he may have been motivated by an ancient legend that said the rulers of India had defeated every foe who ever entered their lands, except for Dionysus, the Greek god, and the mythical hero Heracles. Some historians think the king was simply driven by a lust for war and power. Whatever Alexander's motivation, most of his troops did not share it. They followed him because they were disciplined soldiers. Some may have also been lured by the hope of finding some of the rare treasures that were said to be in abundance in India–a land few people in the West had ever seen.

In the spring of 326 B.C.E., Alexander and his army made the 400-mile trek from Bactria to India. The land then known as India was not the huge sub-continent it is today, but roughly its northern third, and the Macedonians knew little about it. Had they been more familiar with its climate, they probably would not have chosen the beginning of the monsoon season as the time to invade. Heavy rains poured relentlessly for several months, becoming a greater challenge than the humans Alexander had come to conquer.

The first test of Alexander's army came against King Porus (dates unknown), who ruled over land that is today a part of northern Punjab. One

OPPOSITE
I Surrender
King Porus surrenders to Alexander after the Battle of the Hydaspes in this somewhat fanciful 18th century French drawing.

of Alexander's allies, a neighboring king, had requested help battling Porus, his longtime enemy in the struggle over land rights. Alexander agreed. He confronted Porus at the Hydaspes River (now known as the Jhelum River), which flows though India and Pakistan.

The Battle of Hydaspes

The battle of Hydaspes in May 326 B.C.E. is considered one of Alexander's greatest military achievements. To come out the victor, the Macedonian leader had to draw on a number of skills: an understanding of psychology, cool nerve, quick reactions, resourcefulness, command of strategy, organizational ability, and leadership. The discipline of his troops was also of critical importance.

As the Hydaspes swelled from the rains, Porus and his army waited on the opposite bank. In addition to his soldiers and archers, he had more than 100 war elephants. Alexander's army built rafts to cross the river, but because the horses were terrified of the elephants, this was a challenge. If the horses were even to catch sight of the huge beasts during the crossing, it was likely they would jump off the rafts and be swept away by the current.

In pouring rain and thunderstorms, Alexander repeatedly tricked Porus into thinking he was about to attack. He orchestrated large troop movements at crossing points along the river. Night after night, he marched his army along the bank with trumpets blowing. Porus and the elephants would march to meet them on the opposite bank. Then Alexander would retire, leaving the Indians waiting in the rain.

To keep Porus guessing, the Macedonians built up large stores of food and supplies, making it seem that they might be planning to sit out the floods. This in itself conveyed a lack of resolution. Soon, Porus stopped moving his troops every time Alexander moved his. Finally, during a violent thunderstorm on a dark night, the Macedonian army crossed the river. Porus learned of their crossing too late. Catching the Punjabi king's infantry by surprise, the Macedonians immediately killed about half of them.

As he had done in other battles, Alexander avoided a confrontation in the center of the battlefield. He attacked Porus's flank, forcing him to reorganize his forces. He then took advantage of the Indians' confusion, attacking decisively. Alexander lost an estimated 1,000 men; the Indians lost more than twice that many. Alexander's archers also shot the elephants' mahouts, or drivers. The elephants then trampled the Indian soldiers around them. Many of the Indian soldiers retreated, but Porus fought on. From the back of the tallest elephant, the seven-foot-tall king kept hurling

INDIAN WEAPONRY

Indian military experts used swords and spears handmade from the strongest and highest quality steel, an iron that had recently been discovered by Indian blacksmiths. They were also equipped with large, powerful bows and six-foot-long arrows. In addition, they trained horses and elephants to fight in wars. Elephants in the Indian army had metal tips fitted to their tusks.

javelins at the Macedonian soldiers, even though he was bleeding from a deep wound.

Alexander sent a messenger to Porus, who surrendered after eight hours of fighting. According to Michael Wood's account of the legendary story, in his book *In the Footsteps of Alexander the Great*, when the defeated Porus was asked how he wanted to be treated, he replied, "Treat me like a king." Impressed with the Indian king's courage and dignity, Alexander not only restored Porus's kingdom, he enlarged it. The two kings became close friends and Porus's elephant even became an honored hero. On the site of the battle, Alexander founded two new cities. One was called Nicaea, which means victory. The other was named Bucephala, in honor of Alexander's treasured warhorse, Bucephalas (see the box on page 41), who died at the ripe old age of 29, possibly during the battle. Both towns were near Haranpur, in the northern Punjab, northwest of what today is New Delhi, India's capital.

Elephants of War

In India, Alexander's army had to devise new strategies to deal with war elephants. This manuscript illustration of elephants in battle is from a 15th century French history book.

Turning Back

During June and July, the army traveled through the Punjab (it means "land of five rivers") region of India. The soldiers crossed four of the five rivers, and as they went, their difficulties worsened. Alexander did not often underestimate his human enemies, but in the summer of 326 B.C.E., he did underestimate nature. He had no idea how unbearable the experience of the Indian monsoons would be for his men. For more than two months, it was hellishly hot, and the unceasing rain was accompanied by thunder and lighting. Some of the rivers, swollen with the torrents, burst their banks and flooded the land around them. The tired soldiers marched through thick mud. Their clothing, never having a chance to dry out, began to rot and fall apart. To prevent rust, they were forced to scour all their iron equipment daily.

To cross the rivers, Alexander's troops made rafts out of their tents by stuffing them with straw and piled their belongings on top. Some soldiers were swept away by the raging waters. Crocodiles that infested the rivers killed others. The rain also caused poisonous snakes to come out of their holes looking for higher ground. Many soldiers died of snake bites.

The relentless rain was not the only problem. The soldiers had believed India would be an easy land to conquer, but Porus warned them that ahead of them lay large and powerful kingdoms with huge armies and thousands of elephants. They also discovered that the Encircling Ocean was nowhere near. After eight hard years of nearly unending marching and combat, the soldiers had little will or energy to go on. Along with their patience, the hooves of their horses had been worn thin by steady marching. Even their armor had become nearly useless from wear.

When they reached the fifth and last of the Punjab rivers, the Hyphasis (now the Beas) River, the soldiers had finally had enough. Alexander pressed to continue east across the river, but his troops refused. Now clearly aware that their leader was never going to willingly stop marching and fighting, they refused to carry on. The Macedonian army, traditionally democratic, was acting within its legal rights in mutinying. All troops had the right to suggest a plan of action and bring it up for a vote. The king was elected by the army and could also be removed by the army. Alexander had no choice but to go along with their wishes. Even so, for two days the king tried to change their minds . He threatened to continue on alone. When that failed, he closed himself off inside his tent and brooded in silence, much like Achilles in *The Iliad*. This tactic had worked before to sway his troops, but not this time.

A soldier named Coenus, who had been the hero of the battle at the Hydaspes, acted as the army's spokesperson and clearly let Alexander know that his soldiers had had enough and did not want to go on. Finally, Alexander relented, managing to save face when his seers read the omens from the gods, which warned against continuing east. By emphasizing that the gods, not the soldiers, had forced him to return, Alexander was also able to maintain his authority. In September 326 B.C.E., for the first time in his military career, Alexander the Great turned back.

By Land and Sea

For their departure, Alexander had a fleet of 1,800 ships built in just two months, under the supervision of his admiral and old friend Nearchus (c. 360–c. 300 B.C.E.). Carpenters used simple tools to construct both riverboats and vessels that could be taken to sea. In November, Nearchus led the fleet south from the Hydaspes River toward the Indus River and the Indian Ocean.

The main part of the army marched alongside the river, at the same pace as the ships. The army, which now included elephants, had to fight hostile groups along the way. They fought with the ferocious Mallians, who lived east of the Acesines (today the Chenab) River. During one fight, Alexander received a serious wound when an arrow pierced his chest. The army reached the port town of Patala (near today's Hyderabad) in July 325 B.C.E. After resting with his troops and exploring some nearby river channels, Alexander began to plan out his return trip to Babylon. First, he instructed a trusted general, Craterus (c. 362–321 B.C.E.), to take a more northern route west, the easiest way back. Craterus traveled with the elephants and about a third of the troops, including older or sick soldiers.

At the same time, Nearchus and nearly 20,000 men set sail west from the mouth of the Indus River, up the coast into the Persian Gulf. They explored the northern shore of the Arabian Sea and the Persian Gulf, seeking the mouth of the Tigris and Euphrates Rivers. Today it is not easy to reconstruct their voyage, as it was not possible at that time to measure distances at sea. Many historians believe the fleet traveled this route to open up a sea trade route between Persia and India. To accomplish this, they would have had to chart the coast and make maps of landing sites and wells. In fact, trading routes did open up or were reinforced after this voyage. One important trade route linked western India to port cities of Egypt via the Red Sea.

Death in the Desert

Alexander himself marched his remaining army of 30,000 men west to Turbat, Pakistan, and then, instead of continuing west as would have been expected, he headed south toward the Indian Ocean. The plan was for Alexander to meet up with Nearchus there, and probably again at various points along the way westward. The fleet would supply the land troops with grain and provisions and the troops

CONNECTIONS >>>>>>>>>>>>

The Shape of a Delta

The fourth letter of the ancient Greek alphabet, delta, corresponds to our letter D and is written as a triangle. The Greeks also gave the name *delta* to a wedge-shaped island formed by sediment at the mouth of a river, and English borrowed this word from the Greeks.

would provide wells and protection for the fleet whenever it needed to come ashore for fresh water. Alexander's decision to follow the coast rather than return up to Turbat and go west from there was not a fortunate one. It took the army through miles of some of the world's worst deserts, including the Makran Desert that borders the north end of the Indian Ocean, as well as the region of Gedrosia, which lies northwest of the Makran.

As with so many other events of Alexander's career, historians disagree about many aspects of this march. They are not sure whether Alexander knew how difficult this crossing would be. Some believe he did know and wanted to prove that his army could do what others had failed to accomplish. Others believe he had no idea and that local guides who were hostile to the Macedonians may have intentionally misinformed them. Other historians believe the disaster was the result of an unfortunate series of events and that Alexander's legendary luck finally failed him.

The march was a disaster because the fleet failed to meet with the army, as planned. The army, which had set out before the fleet, marched to the coast and reached the rendezvous point. There, the troops on land waited for the fleet, which never showed up. No one knew why. They later discovered the ships had waited an extra week for the monsoons to die down and were further delayed by headwinds.

The soldiers had been depending on the fleet to

Desert Dangers

If Alexander meant to meet up with his fleet and its commander, Nearchus, at either Pasni or Gwadar, further along the coast, that mission failed. The troops were left to make a death-defying trek west across the desolate Makran Desert and up into the Gedrosian Desert. From Pasni it took days by camel train to reach the scorched seaside enclave of Gwadar, where Alexander dug wells.

Today the westward trip might take three days at least, in a landscape still reminiscent of a barren world on another planet. There is no fresh water to be found between the two towns. Along the way, stark, dry ridges jut into the sky. Deep, drifting dunes make walking nearly impossible and camels are the only practical means of transportation. The vegetation is sparse. The sun burns and rains rarely fall. At a place called Sur Bandar, crude straw huts hug the shore and the boats of fishermen dot the sea's surface— the only hint of a more modern world.

The modern world is apparent, however, in today's Pasni and Gwadar, though both were pillaged and burned in 1581 c.e. by Portuguese explorers. Gwadar is striving to become a major seaport on the level of its neighbor to the east, Karachi, Pakistan, and Pasni today is well-known to the United States Army. Since the September 11, 2001, terrorist attacks, the military and allied forces have been using Pasni's commercial airport as an air base, as they also did during World War II.

supply them with food, and soon used up the food supplies available in this barren region. They could not return the way they had come, because they had stripped the land through which they had just traveled. Without food, they could not remain at the meeting point to wait for the fleet, especially since they feared it had been destroyed by a storm or an enemy attack. At Gwadar, instead of continuing to march along the coast, Alexander led his army inland. This fateful decision meant that, unbeknownst to them, they would march through the worst part of the desert.

Alexander began his desert march with somewhere between 10,000 and 70,000 people. As always, women, children, craftsmen, and others traveled with the soldiers. Three-quarters of them perished along the way in a trek that took about two months. The whole entourage suffered severely from starvation, thirst, and disease. Flash floods and poisonous snakes wiped out many. Those who were too sick and exhausted to continue were left behind to die. Alexander shared these hardships, and often, to set an example, dismounted from his horse and walked.

It is believed that more soldiers died from hunger and thirst during the crossing of the Gedrosian Desert than in all of Alexander's battles in Asia. But finally, at the end of 325 B.C.E., the survivors reached Carmania in eastern Persia (today's Kerman in south central Iran). There, they reunited with Nearchus's fleet and Craterus's troops and a great celebration ensued.

Rebuilding an Empire

Alexander returned to Susa early in 324 B.C.E., where he discovered that some parts of the Persian Empire had started to rebel during his Indian campaigns. Several satraps had recruited private armies and had been abusing their powers, as if they had expected Alexander would never return.

Alexander took quick and decisive steps to regain control He executed the rebellious satraps, as well as a number of soldiers from the garrison of Media (now part of northwest Iran) who had plundered temples and tombs. Persian rebel leaders who had been captured by Craterus were also executed. At the same time, the newly returned king began a number of projects aimed at improving trade and expanding the empire's routes of commerce. He had wells dug in dry areas and ordered the building of all-weather roads and bridges—although these plans were never realized before his death and were abandoned afterward as others took control of his lands. He gave large rewards to surviving soldiers who had remained loyal to him and also repaid the debts many of his soldiers had incurred.

ADOPTED MOTHER

One of Alexander's closest friendships was with Sisygambis, the mother of King Darius III of Persia. After being abandoned by her son as he fled the battlefield at Issus (see page 19]), Sisygambis had fully expected death for herself, along with the Darius's wife and children. When Alexander instead treated the royal family with kindness and honor, Sisygambis gained an unexpected respect for the conqueror and a friendship was born.

Over the years, Alexander visited Sisygambis when he could and sent her many gifts. He addressed her as "mother." When Alexander died, the depth of their bond was truly revealed. Upon receiving the news of his death, Sisygambis turned her face to the wall. She remained there, fasting, until she died of starvation.

In an attempt to unite his eastern and western subjects, Alexander organized a mass marriage. He had about 90 of his military officers marry daughters of Persian aristocrats. A sumptuous banquet was held for 9,000 people. Held in March 324 B.C.E., the event was intended to develop a greater spirit of cooperation between Macedonians and Persians.

Alexander set an example by taking his second and third wives, first Parysatis (dates unknown) and then Stateira (c. 340–320 B.C.E.), Darius's daughter. Marrying Stateira added legitimacy to his claim of kingship of the Persian Empire. Alexander's closest companion, Hephaestion, married another of Darius's daughters. Alexander also offered a monetary reward to soldiers who married Persian wives; about 10,000 of his men took advantage of the offer.

In another bold move, the king announced that he was releasing older and injured Macedonian veterans from military service and replacing them with 30,000 Persian young men who had been studying the Greek language and Macedonian methods of fighting. The army, who still considered the Persians barbarians, protested, saying if anyone was dismissed, they would all leave. In response, their ruler again made a stirring speech, this time reminding the soldiers of their glorious victories under him and accusing them of deserting their king. The speech, sometimes called the Oath of Alexander, turned things around yet again. The soldiers withdrew their threat of mutiny.

Alexander discharged about 10,000 men and gave them large bonuses. He provided them with extra money to return to Greece and promised to educate their Persian children. He also had 13 of his most outspoken critics executed without a trial.

Alexander also integrated new troops that arrived from Macedonia with the Persian soldiers. The Macedonians were placed in the front with spears and the Persians, carrying swords and javelins, marched in rows behind them. The Romans later adopted this arrangement, which gave their soldiers greater mobility.

Best Friend

This colossal bronze head of Hephaestion, Alexander's lifelong friend, was probably made by the sculptor Polyclitus in about 324 B.C.E.

The main purpose of the integration of Macedonians and Persians in the army (and also of the mass marriages) was to replace Macedonians with Asians for military and administrative purposes. In addition, the children born of such unions would be of mixed blood, with loyalty to no one but their commander-in-chief.

Death of Hephaestion

In October 324 B.C.E., Alexander's dearest friend, Hephaestion, became ill and died in Ecbatana. Devastated by the death, Alexander ordered Hephaestion's doctor killed, then sat with his best friend's body for three days, never leaving his side. He spent a fortune on a grandiose funeral, which included 3,000 participants in the traditional funeral games. These games included contests in literature and athletics, and emulated the games organized by Achilles for his friend Patroclus, who was killed in the Trojan War. The ceremony, for which a gargantuan funeral pyre was built, took place in Babylon.

After this loss, Alexander's health began to decline and many of his war injuries started to bother him. Some historians believe he had become an alcoholic and that frequent drinking bouts further undermined his health.

It was at this time that Alexander petitioned Greece to confer upon him the status of a god. Although this honor was sometimes granted to Greek rulers after their death, most people, including Alexander's soldiers and the Greeks back home, found the king's request absurd. Some of his

Legendary Friendship

Alexander met Hephaestion when they were boys in Macedonia. The two friends studied together with Aristotle and remained extremely close during their entire lives. Alexander and Hephaestion saw themselves as contemporary versions of Achilles and his dear friend Patroclus, whose brave deeds were chronicled in *The Iliad* (see page 7).

Both pairs of friends have been called homosexual heroes. In ancient Greek culture, sexual relations were common among male friends and it would not have been out of the ordinary for them to be lovers. There was no word in the ancient Greek language for *homosexual* or *bisexual*, as the Greeks did not group people by sexual preference.

Alexander's name for Hephaestion was Philalexandros—"friend of Alexander." Hephaestion's great rival, General Craterus, rated merely the title of Philobasileus, "friend of the king."

Hephaestion was not a great military leader, but probably had gifts for diplomacy and logistics. Although some historians have portrayed him as a man who always agreed with his king, it is more likely that he had great freedom to speak his mind to Alexander, partly because his skills and those of Alexander were complementary, not competitive.

At the time of his death in Ecbatana in 324 B.C.E., Hephaestion was the second most powerful man in Alexander's empire. Alexander died just eight months after his lifelong companion.

countrymen thought Alexander was going insane and even Aristotle criticized him openly. Nevertheless, the Greeks ultimately granted the request, probably because of all the money Alexander had sent them. But their ongoing criticism of him at home showed they did not really believe he was a god.

Back to Babylon

In April 323 B.C.E., Alexander returned to Babylon, which he planned to establish as the capital of his empire. There, he devoted himself, for the first time, to the administration of his vast domain, which stretched from Greece to India.

He had high hopes for his empire. He wanted to create the kind of government that Aristotle championed—rule by a benevolent "philosopher king" (see the box, left). He attempted to instill among his subjects the feeling that they were citizens of a united world, rather than just members of their own nation or culture. He wanted to establish during his reign an era of cooperation, hoping to unite and strengthen his empire by developing a common culture—Greek culture, although with some Persian influences. He gave his Persian cadets instruction in Greek literature and encouraged his eastern subjects to become more like the Greeks and Macedonians.

Alexander also had many ambitious plans. Believing that commerce would help unite his empire, he intended to make Babylon its commercial center. He laid plans to build docks along the Euphrates River at Babylon and to clear and dredge the river to the Persian Gulf. He also planned to colonize the eastern shore of the Persian Gulf and to circumnavigate and explore Arabia. He may have been preparing to invade Arabia and, from there, to conquer the entire North African coast.

Death at 32

Alexander was never to see his grandiose hopes and plans fulfilled. In the early summer of 323 B.C.E. he fell ill, and about 10 days later, on June 10, just before his 33rd birthday and nearly 13 years after becoming the king of Macedonia, Alexander died.

The similarity between his death and Hephaestion's led to suspicions that both were the victims of poisoning. Some historians suggested that Alexander's cupbearer might have been the culprit, spurred on by his father, Antipater (c. 398–319 B.C.E.), the king's Macedonian chancellor. By this time in his life, there was no shortage of enemies or rivals who would have wanted to see Alexander dead. However, most historians today

PHILOSOPHER KING

In his book, *The Republic*, Aristotle's teacher, Plato (427–347 B.C.E.), wrote about the views of his own teacher, Socrates (469–399 B.C.E.). Socrates and Plato believed that an ideal society can only exist when philosophers are kings or kings are philosophers. They defined a philosopher as a person who seeks to understand the essence of things instead of being interested only in their appearances. A philosopher king would be a wise leader motivated by a desire for wisdom, justice, temperance, and goodness in leading his people.

Death of a King
This scene from a 15th century French illustrated manuscript shows Alexander the Great's funeral carriage and gold coffin. The Macedonians spent a year making it after their great leader's death.

agree that Alexander died from disease. The most recent scholarship suggests it was an infectious disease, perhaps typhoid fever, made worse by stress, multiple wounds, endemic malaria, occasional heavy drinking, and exhaustion.

Even though many soldiers had become disillusioned with Alexander, most still loved their leader. They sat outside his tent as his condition deteriorated. The day before he died, his soldiers marched past his deathbed, honoring their great leader. According to Michael Wood's *In the Footsteps of Alexander the Great,* as well as many other sources, the ancient Greek historian Arrian claimed that despite his pain and weak condition, Alexander made eye contact with each of his men as they marched past.

Alexander's remarkable 13-year reign solidified his place in history. But the great conqueror failed to establish a stable empire. Although his first wife, Roxane, was pregnant with a son at the time of her husband's death, Alexander the Great did not designate a successor. In the last moments of the great king's life, his generals asked him to whom he wanted to leave his empire. Many sources, including *In the Footsteps of Alexander the Great* by Michael Wood, provide Alexander's deathbed answer. His reply was, "*to kratisto*"—to the strongest. Alexander shrewdly predicted that his generals would fight one other for control of his kingdom, and he was right. The intrigue and ferocious power struggles among the *diadochi,* or successors, would last for more than a generation.

Intrigue in Alexandria

Alexander's coffin was first buried in the Egyptian capital of Memphis. Later, it was reburied at the center of ancient Alexandria. At that spot, known as the Sema (a word that referred to the place where Alexander's mausoleum was), the city's two grandest streets—colonnaded and each reportedly 200 feet wide—intersected. But as the city grew, its center shifted and knowledge of the tomb's exact location was lost. The last record of its whereabouts is dated in the fourth century C.E. So far, the ongoing search for it has been fruitless.

Recent underwater excavations in Alexandria's old harbor have provided promising clues. Archaeologists now believe that the search should take place much further east in the city than originally thought. They say the old city center was probably in the region of what is now 19th century cemetery grounds. Intriguing evidence has actually been found in the area they suggest, including the vestibule of a royal tomb designed in the Macedonian style and sculpted from high quality alabaster.

After Alexander's death, the Macedonians spent a year creating a magnificent funeral carriage. His body was embalmed and placed in a solid gold coffin, which was carried under a golden, jewel-encrusted model of a temple. A gold statue of the Greek goddess of victory, Nike, stood on the roof of the carriage. At the funeral march, his soldiers followed the carriage, which was pulled by 64 mules wearing golden bells. Road builders went ahead of the spectacular funeral train. As the procession traveled west across 1,000 miles of Asia, its fame spread. Crowds gathered in every city along the way to watch the procession pass.

The destination of Alexander's body was Macedonia, but it never reached his home. Ptolemy (372–283 B.C.E.), Alexander's friend and the new pharaoh of Egypt, seized the carriage and took it to Alexandria, where it was placed in a special tomb. The exact location of Alexander's tomb, like so many of the facts of his life, is hotly contested. Many archaeologists have tried to find it, and some still search for it today.

Three Kingdoms

Alexander turned out to be the only individual whose personal authority could hold his huge empire together. Some of his followers, including the rank and file of the Macedonian army, wanted to preserve the empire, but with no successor named and no stable kingship to maintain what he had won, the empire immediately and rapidly began falling apart.

The power conflict among Alexander's generals, who all wanted to carve out vast realms for themselves, lasted about 40 years, from 323 to 280 B.C.E. Through struggles and warfare, three generals, Ptolemy in Egypt,

Seleucus (c. 358–281 B.C.E.), and Antigonus (c. 382–301 B.C.E.), emerged as powerful contenders. Antigonus was initially the most powerful of the new kings, but he was defeated at the battle of Ipsos in 301 B.C.E. This battle among the kings put an end to all hopes of a reunification of Alexander's domains.

From each of these three generals, a major dynasty emerged: the Ptolemies in what had been the Egyptian Empire (Egypt, Syria, Cyprus, the Agean Islands, and parts of Asia Minor) , the Seleucids in what had been the Persian Empire, and the Antigonids in Macedonia and Greece. Eventually, all three kingdoms were overtaken by the military might of the Roman Empire. The Romans ended political Hellenism, but Hellenic culture remained the basis of the civilization of the East even during the centuries of Roman domination.

The Egyptian Empire of Ptolemy was the richest, most powerful, and most stable of the kingdoms—as well as the longest lasting of the three.

CONNECTIONS >>>>>>>>>>>>>>>>>>>>>>>>>>>

Who is Buried in King Philip's Tomb?

In 1977, archaeologists announced an exciting discovery: They had found what they believed to be the tomb of Alexander's father, King Philip II of Macedonia. The tomb was located in what is now Vergina, Greece. The objects in the tomb, which included a gold larnax, or ancient Greek casket, a magnificent set of armor, and a gold wreath, came from the fourth century B.C.E. The lid of the larnax was embossed with a starburst, which was the emblem of the Macedonian royal family.

The body in the tomb had been cremated, but the bones had been carefully wrapped in a purple cloth. Scientists were able to use pieces of the skull to reconstruct the face, and they discovered that the right side of the face was distorted. This provided further confirmation that the body was that of King Philip II, since it was known that an injury had caused him to lose his right eye.

More recent research has revealed that the tomb is most likely not that of Alexander's father, however, but of his half-brother, Philip III Arrhidaeus. Scientists were able to more closely date the artifacts in the tomb, and discovered they were from approximately 317 B.C.E., the year Philip III died. Using a technique called macrophotography, they were able to study the skeleton in greater detail than had been possible when the tomb was first discovered. They determined that the distortions believed to have been caused by the loss of any eye were actually caused by the effects of cremation and reassembly of the bones.

Alexandria became its capital. Ptolemy lived to an old age, and his kingdom was the last dynasty of the Egyptian pharaohs. Egypt reached its height of material and cultural splendor under Ptolemy II Philadelphus, who ruled from 285 to 246 B.C.E. After his death, a long period of war and internal strife followed. In 30 B.C.E., the death of the famous Queen Cleopatra VII, Ptolemy's descendant, marked the end of Hellenistic rule in the region. Egypt became a province of the Roman Empire.

Seleucus, who was given the nickname "the conqueror," seized the largest territory but was murdered before he could achieve his ambition of seizing the vacant throne of Macedonia as well. His kingdom, however, was continued by his heirs. At its largest, the Seleucid Empire stretched from the Aegean Sea to Central Asia. The Seleucid Dynasty founded the most new cities of any monarchy in history. The Seleucids established many Greek settlements throughout their lands, and their empire lasted more than 241 years. By 129 B.C.E., the Seleucid Empire included Palestine, Syria, and Persia. But it continually lost territory over the years because of wars and rebellions, and slowly crumbled to pieces. The empire's decline continued as the Parthians, a nomadic tribe from central Asia, gradually captured all of its territories east of Syria. Its western areas were annexed by Rome in 64 B.C.E.

The Antigonid kingdom of Macedonia was continuously involved in wars with other kingdoms and struggles with the Greek city-states. Because Alexander had drained Macedonia of much of its manpower, it was the smallest and poorest of the three kingdoms. Although it was weak, this empire remained prestigious as Alexander's homeland.

Immediately after the death of Alexander, the generals appointed two kings: Philip III Arrhidaeus (c. 352–317 B.C.E.), son of Philip II and half-brother of Alexander; and Alexander IV, who was an infant at the time. They ruled jointly until Arrhidaeus's murder in 317 B.C.E.. Ultimately, the ruthless Cassander (358–297 B.C.E.) became king of Macedonia in 305 B.C.E.. Cassander was the son of Antipater, the regent of Macedonia during Alexander's campaigns in Persia. To help pave his way to the throne, Cassander married Alexander's half-sister, Thessalonice (346–298 B.C.E.). He had Alexander's mother killed in 316 B.C.E., and in 310 B.C.E. he executed Alexander's widow Roxane and his son Alexander IV, who was 13 years old.

In the great struggle for control in the years between the death of Alexander and his only legitimate heir, many others were killed too. These included not only several of the king's generals but also his sister, his half-brother, his sister-in-law, and a nephew.

PART II
SOCIETY AND CULTURE

Society in Alexander's Empire

Living in Alexander's Empire

Art, Science, and Culture Across the Empire

CHAPTER 4

Society in Alexander's Empire

THE PHILOSOPHER ARISTOTLE ADVISED ALEXANDER TO "play the part of a leader to the Greeks, and of a master to the barbarians, and to care for the former as friends and kinsmen, and treat the latter as beasts and plants" (as quoted by Dutch scholar and author Jona Lendering at his web site www.livius.org). This view of foreigners as barbarians inferior to the Greeks was shared by most of Aristotle's countrymen. Aristotle's most famous student did not agree with this outlook, however. Alexander came to have a great deal of respect for his eastern subjects, and even began to adopt many of their customs. Eventually, Alexander's respect for the Persians became a source of contention between him, his army, and even his closest generals, but he never changed his mind.

The influence flowed both ways: As a result of Alexander's conquests, Greek culture spread throughout the Middle East. His death marks the beginning of what has become known as the Hellenistic age, which lasted for about 300 years. The term *Hellenism* is typically used to describe the influence of Greece on the East, and most scholars have focused on how Greek culture affected the rest of the world. However, there was a great deal of cross-fertilization between East and West, and Greek society was also influenced by Persia during the Hellenistic period.

There were many similarities between the two societies. Both had strong divisions between their upper and lower classes. Both accepted slavery. Women and children had virtually no rights in either society. However, in many ways the two societies were very different. The Greeks worshiped many gods; most Persians believed in a single god. The Greeks spoke one language; the Persian Empire included many different nationalities with different languages. More than a dozen languages were spoken in Asia Minor alone.

OPPOSITE
Macedonian Mask
This is a sixth century B.C.E. gold Macedonian funeral mask from a necropolis (burial city) in Trebeniste. The Macedonians had a sophisticated culture, but were regarded as barbarians by their Greek neighbors to the south.

The governments of Greece and Persia were very different. Greece was not an empire with a single ruler, but rather was a collection of city-states that functioned much like separate nations, each with its own government, laws, and customs. Some, including Athens, were democracies, some were oligarchies (where power was shared by a wealthy aristocracy) and some, such as Sparta, were monarchies. Although the Greek city-states sometimes united to fight a common enemy, they functioned autonomously. Persia was a unified monarchy, with a single, central ruler.

Macedonia: Kingdom with Shared Power

Macedonia, Alexander's homeland, was just north of Greece. Macedonia was a monarchy, but unlike the Persian Empire, where the king had absolute power, the power of the Macedonian king was limited. His primary responsibilities were administrative and military, although he also was in charge of official religious functions. For example, he performed state sacrifices daily, and Alexander did too, every day until his death. The king was also the final judge in any legal appeal.

The king shared his power with the Macedonian assembly. Made up of Macedonian citizens, the assembly was a powerful group that, among other responsibilities, judged cases of treason. Although in theory the king and the assembly shared equally in the government of Macedonia, the power of the assembly was in reality not as great as that of the king. But because the aristocrats controlled large groups of followers, the king needed their support to continue ruling effectively. The most powerful aristocrats were considered the king's social equals.

The Macedonian aristocracy was not based entirely on birth. All men had an equal opportunity to rise in service to the king, who chose his Companions—the elite group of soldiers who served the king directly—based on personal quality and loyalty rather than on family lineage. In Macedonia, the king was expected to listen to his people. The Macedonian people were traditionally allowed to address the king with a great deal of freedom. A soldier addressing the king in the assembly would have to uncover his head, but whatever his rank, he could speak openly and frankly.

One of the most important responsibilities of a new king was to ensure the succession by creating heirs as soon as possible. For this reason, many Macedonian kings had more than one wife. They were also expected to train their heirs in the arts of hunting and warfare.

Strife in the royal family had always been common in Macedonia. There had also traditionally been disputes among the leading aristocrats.

MORE THAN ENOUGH

When Alexander was a boy, his tutor, Leonidas (dates unknown), rebuked him for using too much incense when performing a sacrifice to the gods. He threw an extravagant amount—two fistfuls—of incense on the altar fire and Leonidas criticized him for wasting this valuable commodity. When Alexander captured Gaza, the main spice center for the Middle East, he sent Leonidas a gift of 18 tons of incense. He also sent a note to his former tutor urging him not to be stingy toward the gods.

Macedonian kings were therefore never really safe, even in their own palaces, as this kind of strife often led to plotting, intrigue, and assassination. It became a custom for the kings to station guards both outside and inside the door to their bedroom.

Because the Macedonian kingship was so unstable, princes typically married soon after they turned 20—much earlier than other men in that society. This was to ensure that there would be a male heir available as soon as possible to take the throne in the likely event that it became necessary. When Alexander became king at the age of 20, his advisors tried to convince him to marry and have a child before leaving to invade Persia. He should have taken their advice, since the lack of a clear heir was a major reason why his empire fell apart after his death. It is quite possible, however, that even if Alexander had fathered a son before leaving Macedonia, rivals would have killed the prince.

Persia: Absolute Monarchy

The king of the Persian Empire was an absolute monarch. Known as the Great King or King of Kings, he ruled by divine right (a right conferred by God) and exercised complete control over his subjects. The only limit to his enormous power was that he was expected to follow Persia's customs and was required to consult the highest-ranking nobles before making any important decisions. And yet, because of the king's power, these nobles often simply agreed with the king, no matter what he said.

Although the Persians did not regard their king as a god, everything about him was meant to emphasize his grandeur and superiority. There was lavish pomp surrounding the king and his court. He wore regal purple robes and sat on an elaborately decorated throne.

King Xerxes' Palace
The Persian king was an absolute monarch. One of the many ways he demonstrated his total authority was by building grand palaces, such as the one at Persepolis. This is Hypostyle Hall.

His servants were required to hold their hands in front of their mouths in the king's presence so that he would not be forced to breathe the same air they did. He walked on red carpets that were put out only for him. In sculptures of the king, he was always shown as larger than everyone else.

The king provided a meal each day for about 15,000 nobles, courtiers, and other subjects. This was meant to show his concern for his loyal subjects. It also showed off his enormous wealth. The king himself was hidden from the view of his guests when he ate. All of the king's subjects, including the highest nobles, were expected to prostrate (kneel) before the king, bowing their foreheads to the ground—a practice called *proskynesis*. *Proskynesis* is an example of the kind of cultural difference that existed between east and west. In the later years of his reign, Alexander tried to convince his army to practice this custom and bow down to him, but most of them would not accept it (see the box on page 46). The controversy led to a disastrous rift between Alexander and his men.

Greece: Freedom for Some

One of the most important ideas that has been handed down by the ancient Greeks is that of democracy. Among the many forms of government that emerged in Greece's many city-states was the world's first democracies, where all its citizens had equal rights. Citizens had the freedom to think and to speak as they wished and the right to choose their public officials. Citizens had democratic liberty and political rights, and could own land. However, only one out of every six residents was a citizen.

Society in most of the Greek city-states, even the democracies, was actually based on an economic and military aristocracy. There were

Lively Debate
Public debate and inquiry into the nature of society was a well-established feature in Greek political and social life. Italian Raphael (1483–1520) painted The School of Athens *on the wall of the Vatican Palace in Rome to honor this tradition. This detail shows Greek philosophers Plato and Aristotle.*

inequalities among the citizens and the other two types of residents: foreigners and slaves. Foreigners had no political rights. If a foreigner stayed in a city for longer than a specified period of time, he had to register as a resident alien and pay a tax. Resident aliens might be artisans, merchants, or bankers. They could become wealthy and, with good luck, they could become citizens; but with bad luck, they could also end up as slaves.

Even among citizens in Greece's most prominent democracy, Athens, there was social and economic inequality. Athens was a patriarchal society, meaning that the father controlled the family. Women did not have the same political rights as men. Girl babies were not even fed as well as boys. Married women were practically prisoners in their homes. They could not leave the house except to visit relatives, attend marriages and funerals, and participate in certain religious festivals. A wife sometimes shopped at the market for small purchases. When women went out, they were required to have a male servant or slave chaperone them. Women did not have the right to attend political assemblies or to vote. With few exceptions, they were not allowed to participate in public events at all—not even dinner parties.

Women could not own, inherit, or manage property, or take part in any business deal in which something worth more than a bushel of grain was exchanged. Poor women worked, however, as dressmakers, weavers, and midwives. A woman had to have an official male guardian to protect her physically and legally. Citizen women had recourse to the courts in disputes over legal issues. But they had to have men speak for them. Women had authority only over children and slaves. A woman was responsible for cooking, housework, and spinning and weaving cloth for the family's clothing.

Persia was also a patriarchal society in which women lived very suppressed lives. They took care of the home and were encouraged to

CONNECTIONS >>>>>>>>>>>>

Greek Politics

Many of the political ideals we cherish today came from the Greeks. The word *politics* comes from the Greek word *polis*, usually translated as "city-state" to emphasize its difference from what we today normally think of as a city. The word *democracy* comes from the Greek word *demokratia*, which means "the authority of people."

When Greek civilization began, authority was based on brute force—as it was in most of the ancient world. But the Greeks were the first to ask what the role of a government should be. Some Greek philosophers determined that the state should exist for the benefit of its citizens. Therefore, they reasoned, those citizens had the right to help make decisions. They believed that it was not just a right, but also a duty of every citizen to participate in the government.

have as many children as possible, so that the king's army would always be supplied with soldiers. They were not allowed to see any men other than their husbands. Unlike Greek women, however, they were permitted to own property and could conduct business from their homes.

Class Systems Throughout the Empire

The Greeks, the Macedonians, and the Persians all had class systems. The upper classes of Macedonian society admired the Greeks. The Macedonians had their own language, which may have been similar to Greek, but the upper classes also spoke Greek. They considered themselves to be Greek by blood. At the same time, Macedonia was a rough land with a colder climate, and the Macedonians looked down on their southern Greek neighbors as softer and less hardy than themselves.

The Greeks thought even less highly of the Macedonians, whom they scorned. They considered Macedonia a crude backwater whose people were little better than barbarians.

There were some significant differences between the culture of Macedonia and that of the rest of Greece. Even though Macedonia was a male-dominated society, the queens and royal mothers were greatly respected. This was largely because they came from powerful Macedonian families or from ruling families in neighboring lands. They were given respect because they gave birth to the heirs their husbands needed for their royal dynasties to continue. When the king was away, the royal women sometimes engaged in power struggles with the king's male representatives, as Alexander's mother did.

The favorite pastimes of the Macedonian upper classes were fighting, hunting, and heavy drinking. The king could only get respect from the nobility if he was an expert in all these activities, which was seen as an indication that he would be capable of heading the state. Hunting on horseback was seen as a useful aspect of military training. Alexander loved riding and hunting, and before he became king he probably hunted almost every day. He stalked animals such as bears, lions, and stags that roamed the hills of Macedonia.

Persian society was divided into two classes. We know more today about the lifestyle of Persia's upper classes than about its lower classes. The upper class included the king, the nobility, and the priests. At the head of the upper class was the king. Just below him in power were his chief noblemen. They served as officers and cavalry in the army. The lower class included the majority of Persians, who were laborers. Freemen got paid and

BABBLING BARBARIANS

Aristotle, like all the Hellenes of his time, believed people who did not speak his language were uncouth *barbaroi*, not deserving of any status much better than slave. The Greek word *barbaroi*, the root of the English word *barbarian*, is translated as "babbler" or "jabberer." So all non-Hellenes were considered nothing but babblers—barbarians in the true Hellenic sense.

could choose where they worked. Bondsmen were serfs and slaves, and had little or no choice as to where and for whom they worked.

All of the land in Persia belonged to the king, but the kings gave land holdings to nobles and military leaders. These lands were named in military terms, according to their size. For example, there were "bow," "horse," and "chariot" lands, and the owners of these lands had to provide men and equipment for the army accordingly. One of the smallest parcels, a bow land, was about 52 acres and its lord was expected to supply one archer to the army. Some lords had parcels of many thousands of acres and had to provide much greater numbers of men and equipment.

Serfs and Slaves

Maintaining these estates required a lot of work. Serfs lived on a Persian noble's estate and worked in exchange for some of the crops. These serfs were considered part of the property on which they worked. They were expected to fight for the noble who owned the land, if necessary. If the land changed hands, the serfs and their families remained with it.

Slaves, unlike serfs, could be sold. They were often more highly skilled than serfs. Many were prisoners of war who performed the same trades they had performed before they were captured.

In most of Greece there were no serfs (Sparta was one exception), but there were slaves. Slaves were considered to be their owners' property. They had few rights and could have no family or possessions. Slaves could, however, buy or inherit their freedom.

People ended up as slaves for many reasons. Children who were abandoned by their parents often became slaves, as did enemy soldiers who had been captured. Captives were rarely killed because they were valuable to their captors. How captives were treated depended on whether their families were rich or poor. Rich captives were often sold back to their families, while poor captives typically became slaves. Alexander sent many captured soldiers back to Greece and Macedonia to become slaves.

The lives of most slaves were probably not too different from those of farm workers or servants. An exception was slaves who had to dig in the silver mines in Athens and Macedonia. Their lives were extremely difficult.

The Vast Persian Empire

The Persian Empire had an ancient culture, as old and in some ways as advanced as Greece's. From about 550 B.C.E. until Alexander's time, the Persian Empire was ruled by a dynasty called the Achaemenians. The first and greatest of the Achaemenian kings was Darius I. His rule, which began in 522 B.C.E., ushered in what is known as the Achaemenian era, which continued until Alexander conquered the empire.

By the time Darius I came to power, the Persian Empire had expanded to include a vast territory of diverse populations. It stretched from what is now Turkey in the west to what is now Afghanistan and India in the east. Its northern boundary was the southern part of the former Soviet Union, and in the south it extended to Egypt and the Indian Ocean.

The Persian Empire was the largest, most powerful, and wealthiest empire in the world. The kingdom was nearly 5,000 miles wide from east to west. It encompassed a total of 15 modern countries—a new country was added almost every 10 months. It was wider than the continental United States and spanned parts of three continents.

The Persian Empire united people and kingdoms from every major civilization of the time except China. Its many regions had different traditions, laws, economic conditions, languages, and cultures, which were brought together under one ruler for the first time. At its height, the empire had about 40 million people.

Although Persia was a monarchy, its enormous size made it impossible for one person to govern it effectively. Darius I set up a system of provincial organization, dividing his lands into 20 huge districts, called *satrapies*. Many satrapies were large enough to constitute kingdoms in themselves. Each satrapy was ruled by a local governor, called a satrap.

Satraps were chosen mainly from the persian nobility; many were members of the Persian royal family or trusted friends. A satrap was a powerful figure who ruled over his province like a monarch. However, the kings put measures in place to keep the satraps from having too much power. For example, they put army officers in charge of the military forces stationed in the satrapy and appointed other officials to collect the taxes. Not satisfied to trust this system of shared power, the kings also sent out royal inspectors to keep an eye on the satraps and the other officials.

When Alexander conquered the empire, he allowed most of the satraps and other Persian officials to remain in positions of authority. He usually gave administrative power to the Persians and gave the Macedonians control over the military and the treasury. He also gave peasants the right to make a direct appeal to the king for the first time.

The Persian Empire became rich, in part, through the taxes the kings collected. The annual tax typically amounted to about 10 percent of the people's resources and could be in the form of precious metals, food, or other commodities. Taxes were collected in different ways in different areas. Money was also collected as tribute from rulers of nearby lands in order to preserve peace.

For nearly 200 years before Alexander, the Persians held an annual festival on New Year's Day at the spring equinox, called the Festival of the Tribute. Representatives from all parts of the empire would come to the magnificent royal palace at Persepolis for this grand occasion, many bringing gold and silver by camel. As part of a great ceremony, they would wait in their national dress until they were ushered in to see the king. They would present offerings and gifts to the king, who held court in a great hall whose ceiling was supported by 100 columns.

These revenues, along with the empire's mineral deposits, forests, and other natural resources, made the Persian kings wealthy beyond the imagination of the Greeks or Macedonians. For centuries the kings had stored vast treasures in their palaces. Alexander had virtually all of the Persepolis treasury melted down and recast as coins honoring local kings, beginning with Alexander himself. He set up several mints to facilitate this process, and minted coins became the standard currency throughout Greece and Persia. This helped unify the empire and put huge amounts of coined money into circulation. It also made many of Alexander's soldiers rich. A generous leader, he often showed his appreciation for his troops' loyalty by giving them bonuses and lavish gifts. Some of the soldiers began living like kings themselves.

A Tent Fit for a King

One key difference between the Macedonians and the Persians was the lavish wealth of Persian royalty. Alexander, who lived much more simply than his Persian counterparts, was amazed by the opulence of the royal tent left behind when Darius III fled from the battlefield at the Battle of Issus. It contained a golden throne and bath, gold and silver drinking cups, carpets, jewels, and other treasures. The historians Arrian (85–195 c.e.) and Quintus Curtius Rufus (40–60 c.e.) give an account of Alexander's reaction to this fantastic wealth. As related in Michael Wood's book *In the Footsteps of Alexander the Great,* Alexander remarked, "So this is what it is like to be a king."

Another key difference was the way royalty was addressed in the two cultures. Alexander entered the tent with his close friend, Hephaestion. Darius's mother, Sisygambis, had been left behind when Darius fled. Seeing the two men, she assumed that Hephaestion, the taller and thus more impressive man by Persian standards, must be the king and addressed him as "Alexander." Learning of her mistake, she became afraid, possibly believing that such an insult would cost her life. Many sources, including Robin Lane Fox in his book *Alexander the Great*, provide Alexander's legendary reply. "Do not worry," Alexander told Sisygambis, "He, too, is Alexander."

Royal Road and Trade Routes

Persian kings ruled their diverse peoples efficiently. Darius I built many roads that linked the satrapies. The main highway, known as the Royal Road, extended from the Greek city of Ephesus on the Mediterranean coast to the valley of the Indus River. Their network of roads enabled the Persians to run an efficient postal service. The Royal Road was divided into 111 post stations—each equipped with fresh horses. The king's messengers changed horses at each station.

The road system facilitated the operation of the Persian Empire and enabled the Persian kings to keep abreast of developments throughout their lands. The existence of these roads also made it easier for Alexander to conquer the empire. Later, the roads enabled the Greek influence to spread more quickly through the Persian Empire.

Macedonian mail riders used the Royal Road, just as the Persians had, to transport mail. Riding horses and special camels bred and trained for speed, they carried mail back and forth between the soldiers in Persia and the Macedonian capital, Pella. The Persian Royal Road was also an important trade route. For centuries, tradesmen had led their caravans across dangerous deserts, mountains, and steppes to sell their goods at

CONNECTIONS >>>>>>>>>>>>>>>>>>>>>>>>>>>>>>>>>>>

Neither Snow nor Rain . . .

The Persian road system was extremely efficient. The Greeks were impressed with a practice called *angareion*, which involved riders exchanging horses along the way in a sort of relay race. The Greek historian Herodotus, in his *The Histories*, wrote of this practice, "There is nothing mortal which accomplishes a journey with more speed than these messengers, so skillfully has this been invented by the Persians." (A full translation of *The Histories*, in which this material can be found, is available at ancienthistory.about.com/library/bl/bl_text_herodotus_8.htm).

A more recent form of this relay was the Pony Express, which delivered mail from Missouri to California in the United States from early 1860 through October 1861.

Herodotus's next words are familiar to most people living in the United States: "Neither snow nor rain nor heat nor gloom of night stays these couriers from the swift completion of their appointed rounds." These words are inscribed on the general post office building in New York City, and have become the unofficial motto of the United States Post Office.

CONNECTIONS >>>>>>>>>>>>>>>>>>>>>>>>>>>>>>>>>>

The Precious Pearl

According to Greek mythology, when Aphrodite, the goddess of love and beauty, shed tears of joy they turned into pearls. To the ancient Egyptians, pearls were precious because they represented one of their most important goddesses, Isis, whose domain was magic, medicine, healing, and the rituals of everlasting life.

Historians believe that the pearl was most highly valued first by the cultures of the ancient Middle East. From the time of the Achaemenid kings, the Persians had control of the Persian Gulf, one of the earliest and most abundant sources of these gems. which are made by oysters. So it is not hard to imagine that as the new king of Persia, Alexander must have had his choice of the finest pearls.

From Persia, the love of pearls spread to the Mediterranean where, by the first century B.C.E., it became almost fanatical. Ancient pearl-encrusted objects have been unearthed at digs throughout the ancient Roman Empire, down into North Africa, and as far north as northern France. Pearls were more valuable and sought after than gold, and a single piece of pearl jewelry might be worth many thousands of today's dollars.

By the time the Arabs controlled the region of the Persian Gulf, pearls were being transported not only along the Silk Road but by sea as well. In the first century B.C.E., Julius Caesar proclaimed pearls off-limits to anyone but the Roman rulers, and at the peak of the British Empire no common subject was allowed to wear pearls either. By the 1500s, Seville, Spain, and Lisbon, Portugal, had become the centers of the pearl trade, and these cities overflowed with the finest specimens from the Persian Gulf, India, and other parts of the East.

During the late 1600s, pearls began to lose their distinctive specialness in Europe and elsewhere. The custom of lavish adornment with pearls gave way to much more modest displays as religious and political values became more conservative.

Today, a string of pearls is a more common piece of jewelry and may cost only a few hundred dollars. Just looking at a such a simple piece of jewelry, not many would guess the pearl's long and prestigious past.

CONNECTIONS >>>>>>>>>>>>>>>>>>>>>>>>>>>>>>>>>

Traveling Across Time

The long caravan that followed Alexander traveled 11,000 miles back and forth across the Persian Empire. This moving city used the same roads that were later traveled by the Romans, Genghis Khan (c. 1162–1227 B.C.E.), Marco Polo (1254–1324 B.C.E.), and, later still, by British soldiers during World War II.

Roads that branched out from the Royal Road linked all parts of the empire. One branch connected Babylon and Ecbatana, crossing the Royal Road near Opis and continuing to the Far East. This route between the Mediterranean Sea and China became part of what is known as the Silk Road during the first century B.C.E. The first users of this important trade route, which actually included four different roads, probably lived between 1000 and 500 B.C.E.

One of the Silk Road's most famous travelers was Marco Polo, a merchant from Venice, Italy. He first traveled along this route when he was 17 years old. He described the exotic East in a book that remains one of the most famous travel books of all time, *The Travels of Marco Polo*. The book added a great deal to what was known of Asian geography and culture and introduced many Westerners to Asian culture.

New ideas also traveled the Silk Road. Believers spread both Buddhism and Islam along its route. Technologies such as printing, paper making, ceramic glazing, glass blowing, and wine making were carried between East and West. New foods, such as noodles, which food historians believe originated in Persia, were also introduced to the world via the Silk Road.

Merchants traveled the Silk Road in caravans of camels. Besides silk, which came from China, they used this route to transport many kinds of goods, including gold and silver, rubies and jade, textiles, ivory, spices, furs, ceramics, and bronze weapons. Salt, which for many years was worth as much as gold, was another important Silk Road product. The city of Salzberg in Austria originated as a salt mining center along the Silk Road.

market towns. These goods included perfumes, incense, gold, jewelry, pearls, crafts such as silver drinking cups, furs, many types of weapons, horses from Assyria, and cattle from Mesopotamia.

During the Hellenic period, most trade was local, between villages and the nearest cities. But there was a tremendous increase in trade between East and West. This was due, in part, to the universal currency and the new coins that had been put into circulation, as well as to the establishment of many new towns and ports. Another important factor was the adoption of Greek throughout the lands Alexander controlled as the language used for trade and diplomacy. Having a common language had a major impact on commerce. Prior to this innovation, confusing mistakes frequently occurred because financial and business transactions were conducted through interpreters. With a uniform currency and language, commerce was greatly simplified.

Increased economic activity throughout the ancient world relieved, for a time, some of the economic difficulties that had threatened Greece. Years of fighting among the city-states had caused the farmers (who were required to serve as soldiers in wartime) to neglect their farms, and for a time food was scarce. The economic boom sparked by Alexander's conquests helped relieve this crisis, at least temporarily. Besides increased trade, war spoils also helped. Alexander divided Persian riches among the Greek towns and city-states that had supported the invasion. As one of the leading powers, Athens received a large amount of silver, gold, and luxury items as its share of the war loot.

A new demand arose in the West for goods such as spices that were not produced in the Mediterranean region. Other goods traded between East and West were building materials such as lumber and asphalt, frankincense, myrrh (an aromatic gum resin used to make perfume and incense), gold, metals, gems, grain, horses, oil, pearls, silk, foods, and wine. Wars had created an unprecedented demand for iron. Buying and selling slaves was also an important part of Hellenistic trade.

Luxury goods were imported from India, Africa, and Arabia, and usually were carried by Bactrian (two-humped) camels, traveling in caravans. Fine embroidery, carpets, tapestries, stones, and jeweled vases came from Babylon, where the knowledge of dyes was very advanced. Trade was also facilitated by the ports Alexander established. Basic items, such as grain, raw materials, and manufactured goods, were usually shipped by sea. Slaves were also carried in boats. As a result, piracy was a constant problem.

Several regions became prosperous through trade. Phoenicia, located along the Mediterranean Sea in what is modern-day Israel and Lebanon, had many merchants and craftsmen who sold wood, cloth, precious metals, and carvings. The Phoenicians, who were not a warlike people, were also expert shipbuilders and sailors. The people of northern Arabia also grew rich this way. They controlled the main travel routes through the Arabian Desert. Persian merchants with caravans of camels used these routes to carry incense from Arabia to other Middle Eastern lands.

CHAPTER 5

Living in Alexander's Empire

A LOT MORE IS KNOWN ABOUT THE WAY PEOPLE LIVED IN Greece than in the lands that had made up the Persian Empire during Alexander the Great's time. Much of what we know about the people who lived in what had been the Persian Empire comes from the Greeks, whose histories were published many years later. The Greeks did not think highly of the Persians, so it is likely that many of their accounts are biased. Distortion of the facts is a common problem whenever history as written by the victors in war is the only version available.

In both East and West, life was very different for the rich than it was for the poor, and city dwellers had different lifestyles than people who lived in the country.

Greece was not a very fertile region. It was crisscrossed by mountain ranges and only small areas were suitable for farming. Staple crops were cereals. People typically raised goats rather than cows. People also kept sheep, for wool as well as for meat. A Greek city-state included the centrally located city and also the villages and small settlements scattered throughout its territory. Life was similar for people who lived in many of the Greek city-states (with the exception of Sparta, a warlike monarchy where many aspects of life were quite different).

Macedonia was a harsh land with many mountains and lowland valleys. It had greater natural resources than Greece, but life was more difficult there. Most Macedonians were poor farmers, and much of the population lived in small villages and towns. Towns did not have protective walls, and were vulnerable to raids by Macedonia's northern neighbors, the Thracians. In most regions of the Persian Empire, most people lived on farms and in small villages. They kept sheep and raised crops such as wheat

OPPOSITE
What They Looked Like
Greeks and Macedonians wore simple, loosely draped clothing made from wool, cotton, linen, or muslin. This marble relief (c. 323 B.C.E.) shows Alexander's friend Hephaestion and an unidentified woman.

and barley to make bread, sesame seeds for oil, almonds, and figs. Farm goods were broadly available to the public. Some villages only had a few dozen households. For most villagers, the greatest fear was that an army would arrive and take their young men away, along with most of their food, animals, and supplies. Contact with the government was limited to the tax collector, who came once a year. Life probably did not change very much for most villagers after Alexander took over.

Eastern Migration

After Alexander the Great conquered the Persian Empire, many Greeks emigrated to its western regions, drawn by the chance to live more prosperous lives than they could at home, where opportunities were limited. A primary reason that Greek culture spread throughout Mesopotamia and the areas to the west during the Hellenistic period was that so many Greeks moved there. Greeks, as well as people from other cultures, settled in cities such as Alexandria in Egypt and Babylon in Mesopotamia. These Hellenistic cities were centers of trade, science, and the arts, but life was not easy for many of the people who lived in them. There were large gaps between the lifestyles of the rich and the poor. The wealthy lived in splendor and luxury, but most city dwellers lived in miserable conditions. Riots were common, especially in Alexandria.

Many of the people who lived in these cosmopolitan cities integrated Greek and Macedonian customs, art, literature, and lifestyles into their own native cultures. However, most people who lived in the countryside ignored much of this Hellenistic influence.

Greeks also settled in the many towns that Alexander and his successors established throughout the former Persian Empire. Most of the new towns and ports were named after Alexander. They were designed to be centers of administration and trade, as well as strongholds that provided protection to the local inhabitants. They served as outposts to keep the peace and to provide warnings to headquarters in case of local uprisings. Towns were usually built at the junction of important roads and placed where they could overlook the surrounding area. They were established close enough to existing villages to enable the newcomers to associate with the natives, but far enough apart that the Macedonian and Greek settlers could keep to themselves.

The first new colonists were typically older, wounded, or disabled war veterans and Greek mercenaries. Many of the veterans settled down with their war loot and a piece of land. Some had started families with women they met while on the march. Later, merchants, craftspeople, and others joined them.

These new towns were typically built on the Greek model, having schools, offices, shops, a temple, a council chamber, and a gymnasium. Such a town might also have a theater, a fountain, and a monument. It would always have a public square, which was the focus of all Greek cities.

Life in the City

The typical Greek style city was centered around the open market, or agora. City dwellers generally rose at dawn. After washing and eating breakfast, most men would head for the agora (the men did a lot of the marketing). The agora was divided into sections where people sold fish, meat, produce, wine, flowers, and other goods. Fruit vendors would display their best olives and figs at the tops of their baskets and hide the rotten fruit on the bottom. Merchants put the coins they received as payment inside their cheeks so no one would steal them. Many merchants could keep as many as 12 coins in their mouths at a time.

The agora was the main place where men socialized, as well. At the agora, men would gather under columned porches to exchange gossip and discuss the issues of the day. They also socialized at barbershops or at blacksmiths' workshops, which were warm even during cold weather. Small businesses and shops of tradesmen, such as upholsterers, barbers, shoemakers, sculptors, doctors, and moneychangers, were located on the streets coming out of the agora. In one section, horse breeders sold or traded animals. In another, men could hire cooks or day laborers to help in the home or field or drive a chariot. There was also a slave market near the agora.

Training the Children

In many Greek city-states, poor children began helping on the farm or in workshops by the age of 10. If they lived in the city, both girls and boys would learn a trade by helping their parents in their daily work. The more fortunate might become apprentices to skilled craftspeople.

In Persia, children under the age of five were taken care of by their mothers and other female relatives. Children did not see their fathers very often before the age of five because it was thought that it would be too hard on their fathers if the children died. (Infant mortality rates were high.)

Starting at five, life was different for girls and boys in the former Persian Empire. Girls stayed home and learned homemaking skills, such as spinning thread and weaving cloth. They did not learn to read and write, but they did learn how to sing and play instruments. For boys, formal teaching began at the age of five. Boys typically received religious education and training in trades and special skills, and trades were passed down from father to son. Wealthy Persians who did not need to learn a trade were taught to ride horses and to use a bow and arrow. Persian nobles built huge parks and hunted in them.

All children also received training in traditional and family values. They were taught to emphasize strong family ties, to be concerned about their communities, and to accept the authority of the king. They were also taught to tell the truth. Telling a lie was considered to be a grave disgrace.

Marriage and Family

In the Persian Empire before Alexander, many customs were driven by the need for a large army in order to maintain the king's power. Persians were encouraged to marry early and to raise large families. Unmarried adults were looked down upon because people thought they were avoiding their duty. Abortion was considered one of the worst crimes and was punishable by death. In order to produce more children, men were encouraged to practice polygamy (having more than one wife at a time).

Parents chose husbands for their daughters when the girls were about 11 or 12 years old and the boys were about 13 or 14. Girls married at 15, the age at which they were considered adults. Boys were also thought of as adults at 15, but they married a few years later. By the time a boy turned 25, he would probably already have several wives.

When a couple became man and wife, the parents of the bride gave the groom's family a dowry, or material offering. The dowry of a well-to-do girl might include precious metals, household equipment, land, jewelry, money, servants, and slaves. It was customary for the bride to move into the home of her husband's family. Marrying close relatives, such as an aunt or even a brother or sister, was considered fortunate in the Persian Empire, and one reason for this custom may have been to keep the wealth of the dowry in the family.

In most of Greece, the bride's family also provided a dowry. If she were wealthy, this might include land that provided an income, along with personal possessions. A husband was required to maintain the dowry, which could be inherited by the children. If the couple divorced, the husband would have to return it.

A Greek woman's father or guardian would arrange her marriage while she was still a child. Girls married when they were 14 or 15, and men

THREE WIVES

Macedonian and Persian kings practiced polygamy. Alexander married three women, all after leaving Macedonia. The first was Roxane in 327 B.C.E.. Then, in 324 B.C.E., he married both Parysatis, the daughter of a Persian nobleman, and King Darius III's daughter Stateira. All Alexander's marriages were thought to have been politically motivated.

Persian kings carried polygamy much further. Some had as many as several hundred wives, who lived together in their own housing. This group of wives, concubines, female relatives, and servants occupying housing that is specially set aside for them is known as a *harem*.

married at the age of about 30. Unmarried women who were not slaves were rare in ancient Greece. A legal marriage began when the bride went to live in her husband's house. The actual ceremony was the procession to the new house.

When they married, women became the legal wards of their husbands. Monogamy (marriage to only one person at a time) was practiced throughout ancient Greece. The nuclear family structure—a husband, wife, and children living together—was the norm. At different times, other relatives might move in with a married couple.

Soldiering as a Way of Life

Every male Greek citizen was required to serve in either the army or the navy. When they turned 18, Athenian men were trained for two years in military discipline and served as police, prison guards, and on garrison duty. They could be called to fight if a war broke out. The Greeks were disciplined soldiers and were in great demand as mercenaries. One of the reasons that there were so many Greek mercenaries is that soldiering for hire was one of the few ways many Greek men could make a good living. Most fighting was done by citizen-soldiers in small armies.

With water on three sides, the Greeks also maintained a navy. Poorer citizens could become oarsmen in the fleet. Wealthier Athenians who could afford the equipment, which they had to pay for themselves, joined the army as hoplites, or foot soldiers. The hoplite's equipment included helmet, shield, breastplate, shin-guards, sword, and spear. The armor was made of bronze or iron plates sewn onto pieces of leather. Soldiers wore bronze helmets with guards that also protected their cheeks and noses. On top of the helmets they usually had a crest of feathers or horsehair. They wore wool cloaks for warmth.

In Alexander's time, the Athenians elected their generals and admirals. A common soldier in one war might be a general in the next. Armies were made up primarily of infantry. Cavalry did not play a large part, because horses were expensive to maintain and Greece's mountainous terrain made them less practical.

Before Alexander's father, Philip II, came to power, the Macedonian army was primarily made up of poor farmers who served as amateur soldiers during part of the year. Philip turned these amateurs into skilled soldiers, creating a professional army in Macedonia. Under Philip, soldiers trained all year long, making long marches with heavy packs to build their strength. Philip also developed a formidable Macedonian cavalry. As in

Greece, members of the cavalry had to provide and feed their own horses, making this a position for wealthy noblemen.

The strongest military branch in the Persian Empire was the navy, which included about 400 warships built by men from Phoenicia. Military leadership was limited to Persian nobles, but all Persian boys entered the military when they turned 18. Males from ages 15 to 50 could be drafted into the army if they were needed. When they returned, they were expected to marry additional wives and have a lot of children.

Alexander's Entourage

When ancient kings went to war, long caravans followed their armies to provide them with food, supplies, and other services. The greatest fear of most villagers was that an army and all its followers would arrive and take their young men away, along with food, animals, and supplies that most villages could not spare. Hostile armies simply took whatever they wanted. "Friendly" armies, too, expected–or required–local people to provide food and other supplies. Sometimes, as Alexander's army did, they would pay for these supplies.

Alexander normally did not allow ravaging and looting, and rarely took all of a village's resources. But even though he usually bought the supplies he needed, most farmers had practically no surplus to sell. Even if they received money, it was not of much use to them, since there was nothing to buy in the countryside.

Alexander traveled with an enormous "moving city" that stretched for miles. The size of his army fluctuated during the 11 years he was in the East, but of the tens of thousands of people who traveled with Alexander, only about half were soldiers. The rest were employed exclusively to take care of the needs of the troops and civilian entourage. Organizing and transporting the food, water, and equipment necessary for so many people was an incredible logistical challenge. Alexander's massive entourage included:

Animals: Donkeys and mules carried most of the supplies and bulky goods. Later, camels were also used. Cattle were brought along for food.

Architects: Alexander founded dozens of fortified towns throughout the Persian Empire, and needed architects to help design and build them.

Artists and writers: Alexander was a favorite subject for painters and sculptors. He even had his own personal sculptor. He also had an official historian, whose job was to immortalize him by writing about his exploits.

Baggage train: Hundreds of wagons carried siege machinery and other large objects. Wounded soldiers were sometimes carried in these wagons as well. Still, Alexander made only limited use of wheeled transport, because wagons require roads or level tracks, which were limited in most of the regions in which he traveled. The harnesses available at that time for animals to pull wagons were also primitive and inefficient, and wagons were too slow for an army noted for its speed of movement.

Clerks and grooms: Accountants, administrators, clerks, grooms, and slaves were needed to manage the army's funds and carry out day-to-day routines.

Cooks and mess staff: Feeding the army was a full-time job for the large group of people who planned, prepared, and served the food.

Engineers, technicians, mechanics, and tradespeople: About 4,000 engineers, mechanics, boat and bridge builders, sinkers of wells, blacksmiths, carpenters, tanners, and painters created the equipment and artillery the army used. Experts in forestry and soil composition were needed to estimate the position and course of rivers, bays, and gulfs, and to identify sites for possible harbors. Surveyors mapped the lands the army passed through.

Entertainers and athletes: Whenever the troops stopped, there were games and festivals. Athletes competed and poets, dramatists, musicians, singers, storytellers, dancers, acrobats, jugglers, and actors entertained. Construction workers and set painters built and decorated theaters.

Merchants: The market that followed the army was as large as that of a capital city's, with a surprising array of goods for sale. Whenever the caravan stopped, horse traders, jewelers, and other merchants set up little markets to supply the newly wealthy soldiers with things to buy.

Scholars, intellectuals, and philosophers: Lively conversation and learning were as important while traveling as they were at home.

From General to King
Lysimachus (c. 355–281 B.C.E.) a Macedonian general, became King of Thrace. Alexander's army offered many opportunities for advancement to men of talent and ability.

Scientists: Conquering may have been Alexander's number one priority, but collecting knowledge must have been a close second. Mineralogists, zoologists, botanists, and other scientists collected specimens of plants and animals to study. They made important discoveries about the geography, climate, and geology of the East.

Scouts and spies: Making maps and acting as translators were among the duties of scouts and spies.

Seers and diviners: Soothsaying, or reading signs and omens to predict the future, was an important job. Astronomers (more like our present-day astrologers) were also on hand to make predictions and give advice.

Women and children: Women whom soldiers had taken as mates along the way and their children often traveled with the army. Prostitutes were also part of the entourage.

CONNECTIONS >>>>>>>>>>>>

Beauty Is in the Eye

Today millions of dollars are spent on eye makeup and other cosmetics for the sole purpose of enhancing one's looks. Cosmetics was a booming business in Alexander's time too. Even back then eye makeup was an essential tool for looking good. But it had a practical aspect too, which came before its use as a beauty application. In the dry desert climates, eye makeup protected the delicate skin around the eyes, kept off flies whose bites could cause inflammations, and sheltered the eyes from the sun's glare—just as modern football players paint black streaks under their eyes for the same reason.

Greek women also spent hours on facials and often went to bed wearing a "beauty mask." A popular recipe was one whose main ingredient was flour, which would then be rinsed off with milk the following morning. Just as today, these remedies were meant to give the skin a fresh, rejuvenated glow. Like modern women, the ancient ones wanted a smooth canvas on which to apply the many colors of their face paint.

Fashion Statements

Greek people wore simple clothing that they wove from wool or plant fibers, including cotton. They also made clothing from animal skins. The wealthy wore muslin or linen. Both men and women went barefoot indoors and wore a draped garment called a *chiton*, which fell about their body in folds. A woman's *chiton* reached her ankles, a man's reached his knees. The *chitons* were kept close to the body with two belts. Most *chitons* were short-sleeved or sleeveless, as long sleeves indicated the person was a slave or a workman.

Until Alexander's time most Greek men had long hair and beards. In ancient Greece, Rome, and the Middle East, intricately groomed long hair was considered a mark of beauty and caring for it was a time-consuming task that most often only the rich could afford. Slaves and ordinary people, who did not have the time or the money that elaborate hair styles required, commonly wore their hair short. When Alexander joined the Macedonian army, he cut his shoulder-length hair to the neck because he did not want it to interfere with his armor. He also shaved his beard— legend has it that this was to make sure an enemy could not grab him by the chin in close combat. When he became king, he ordered his soldiers to shave their beards as well. From his time on, most Greek men had short hair and stopped wearing beards.

In the Persian Empire, men's beards grew long. They thought it indecent to show any of their bodies other than their faces, so their garments draped from head to toe. Both men and women wore long robes. Wealthy people wore elaborate clothes made of luxurious fabrics, such as imported silk. Wealthy men and women both wore jewelry, including rings, earrings, and bracelets set with precious stones.

The king wore a flowing robe of purple, the traditional color of royalty in ancient times, interwoven with gold threads. He also wore a magnificent crown with precious gems and, frequently, beautiful earrings, chains, and bracelets.

Most Macedonians and Greeks thought Persian clothes too ostentatious. But when he was not in battle, Alexander often wore Persian clothing himself, especially in the later part of his reign. He wore a long robe, cape, sash, and headband in the royal purple and white.

Persian Fashion
Darius I listens to a petitioner in this detail (c. 491–486 B.C.E.) from the palace at Persepolis. Persian men grew their beards long and considered it indecent to show any part of their body (other than their face and hands) in public.

Simple Homes

In many Greek city-states, the wealthy, army leaders, government officials, and leading merchants had large, comfortable homes, fine clothing, and the best food. Everyone else lived very simply. (A notable exception was

Versatile Olive Oil

The Greeks found an amazing number of uses for olive oil. It was used in medicine to disinfect and heal wounds, to maintain metal, as a lubricant, as soap, in religious rituals, to preserve clothing, and as a lamp fuel. Athletes spread it over their bodies as a protection against chilly weather. The Greeks used about 16 gallons of olive oil a year per person. Only about a quarter of this amount was consumed as food.

Although today both Greece and Italy produce large quantities of this fragrant green oil, Spain leads the world in olive oil production. It is still a practical commodity, as modern cold-pressing techniques allow the oil's flavor, color, and nutritional value to be retained for several months without refrigeration.

Cold-pressing is done in many stages, so that the oil is gradually pressed out. The olive oil that comes from the last pressing, called olive foots or olive residue, is inedible. But even at this final stage the oil, as in ancient times, has many uses. Olive residue is an ingredient in soaps and detergents, textiles and medicines, and of course in cosmetics.

Sparta, where the lifestyle even for the wealthy was—spartan.) Although the Greeks built large public buildings, houses were typically small and cramped together in crooked little streets. They were made of materials that could be found locally, such as rough stone, wood, thatch, and adobe bricks that were made from earth and straw that was dried in the sun. Many houses were made of clay bricks and had very small windows.

The center of household activity was in the back, in rooms arranged around an open courtyard. The windows faced into the courtyard. (Today, many Mediterranean houses are built on a similar plan.) In the courtyard was an altar for sacrifices to the gods and a cistern, or tank, to catch rainwater. Water from public fountains had to be carried into the house with jugs, a task that fell to the women or slaves.

The couch was the most important piece of furniture in the Greek home. Couches were used for sleeping, eating, reading, and writing. Plump cushions enabled people to recline in comfort while eating. They used small round tables with three legs, which were portable and low enough to be pushed under a couch when they were not being used. Lamps made of baked earth or metal burned olive oil for indoor lighting. A person going out at night would carry a torch or a lantern made of horn.

In the Persian Empire, raw building materials included mud brick, stone, and timber. Local builders had access to limestone, but did not have granite or marble. Bitumen or mineral pitch, a black, tarry material unique to the Middle and Near East, was used for waterproofing and sealing, as a glue, and as mortar for bricks. Baked bricks were sometimes used to construct forts, temples, and expensive private homes for the nobility and those who worked for the government.

The homes of the wealthy were large and filled with expensive objects and elaborate furnishings. They often had landscaped courtyards and were surrounded by high walls of stone or brick. Zoroastrianism, the largest religion in the Persian Empire (see page 94), encouraged maintaining arbors, orchards, and gardens, and gardens with roses, shade trees, and citrus or pistachio trees were common. Many gardens also had ponds and fountains. Some of the kings of the Persian Empire planted and maintained trees in their own gardens.

The houses of poor people were much more modest. A typical house was a rectangular, two-story structure. The house was often divided into separate living quarters, and members of one or more extended families lived under the same roof. They used stairs or ladders, placed both inside and outside the house, to get to the second floor.

Most houses were built of unbaked mud bricks. Some were built on a foundation made of fired bricks or stone. The roof was made of timber beams, which were covered with three layers of material: reed matting, then a layer of lime, and finally a thick layer of mud. The ground floor was earth, covered by reed matting or swept smooth. The top floor might be covered with wool carpet, animal skins, or felt blankets.

Simple Food

Macedonians and Greeks ate simply. Bread was the main part of their diet, baked from barley imported into Greece from the Persian Empire or, for wealthier people, wheat. A family could buy its bread from small bakery stands or make it at home. Wives or household slaves ground the grain, shaped the dough, and baked the bread in a pottery oven that was heated by charcoal.

Greeks also ate vegetables, olives, fruit, and goat cheese. Fish was a popular food in this coastal nation. Wealthier people ate baked turbot, steamed bass, fried shrimp, and smoked herring, as well as squid, eels, and sardines. Vegetables included beans, cabbage, lentils, lettuce, and peas. On special occasions, roasted sheep might be served. Dishes were flavored with garlic and onions. The Greeks also used salt, which they took from the sea.

Only the wealthy could afford to eat meat regularly. Most people enjoyed it only occasionally. For some, meat was only available when the state provided it as part of animal sacrifices during religious festivals. It was grilled over coals on a pottery brazier, a dish shaped much like a modern picnic grill that contained burning charcoal. Meat was easier to come by in Macedonia, which had a lot of forests. Wild boar and deer were part of the

BEDBUG SPICE

The spice known as coriander, native to Greece, is actually the seeds of the cilantro plant. Its name comes from the Greek word *koris* or bedbug, because the Greeks thought the leaves and the unripe seeds of the plant smelled like bedbugs when they were crushed!

How Sweet It Is

Although sugar was being used in India probably as early as 800 B.C.E., it took its sweet time traveling west into the Persian Empire and beyond. Initially the ancient Greeks and Romans used sugar primarily as a medicine. But Alexander was probably familiar with its taste in a more pleasant context. The royals and other of the most wealthy Greek and Macedonian families also coveted it as a food.

It was only in the 10th century that the use of sugar began to spread more deeply into Europe. By then, Venetian traders were becoming fabulously rich importing sugar along with silks and spices such as nutmeg and cloves from the Far East. These same powerful merchants introduced sugar (as well as the spices they had imported) to the Crusaders, who took passage on Venetian ships bound for the Middle East in the 11th century. The Crusaders in turn carried sugar back with them when they returned to Europe. But for the next 400 years it remained a rare treat that only the wealthiest could afford. Finally, the exotic sweet reached the New World when Christopher Columbus took sugar cane there on one of his subsequent expeditions.

One of the best forms of sugar has its roots in the Arabic culture. The Arabs crystallized sugar as a sweet treat they called *qandi*—from which we have our English word "candy."

Macedonian diet. People in Sparta also ate more meat than those in the other Greek city-states.

Everything was washed down with wine, mainly from local vineyards, diluted with water. The Greeks drank both white and red wine. The average Greek household produced much of what it needed to survive, including cheese, bread, vegetables, olives, and wine. They could also purchase staples from local markets. Wine, oil, grain, fruits, and vegetables were kept in large clay jars.

Olives, another staple of the Greek diet, were eaten fresh or pressed into olive oil. The Greeks poured olive oil over raw vegetables and bread and used it as an ingredient in sauces. With a climate that was excellent for growing olive trees and grape vines, the Greeks made superb olive oil and wine.

A typical Greek breakfast was made up simply of bread and wine. Many Athenians had a light lunch in the mid-morning, often eating the leftovers from their dinner of the night before. The agora closed at noon, and men might purchase sausages and pancakes covered with honey from a local vendor for lunch. Dinner was the primary meal.

The Greeks ate everything other than soup with their hands. Food was cut into bite-sized pieces before it was served. In between courses, people wiped their hands on a piece of dough or bread. They later gave this to the family dog to eat. For dessert, they ate figs, nuts, and sticky pastries, which the Greeks invented.

In the Persian Empire, the typical diet of the lower classes included barley, dates, milk, and cheese. Sesame oil rather than olive oil was the main cooking oil. Because of their extensive trade with outlying parts of the empire, the people in the Persian Empire had an abundance of wheat, meat, wine, honey, citrus fruits, and dried fish. They imported spices from India and had a much spicier diet than did the Greeks. Most people in the Persian Empire believed that too much food would make them weak and overweight. They generally ate only one meal a day, but that one meal would often stretch out to take up much of the day.

The ancient Persians also developed farming and animal husbandry techniques that have lasted through the centuries. They introduced new crops, including barley, alfalfa, and rice, throughout their empire. They also may have been the first to domesticate chickens.

Greek Gods

The Greeks and Macedonians worshiped hundreds of gods and goddesses and sacrificed to them. The most important were the 12 great Olympian gods, so called because they were believed to live on Mount Olympus in northern Greece, the region's highest mountain. Different gods presided over different aspects of life. Alexander worshiped and sacrificed to many gods, including Zeus, the king of the gods, and Athena, who had been the patron deity of his maternal ancestor Achilles.

In addition to the Olympians, people in different regions practiced local faiths, which involved worshipping various lesser gods and goddesses, including nymphs (minor nature goddesses, typically pictured as beautiful maidens), naiads (nymphs who lived in bodies of fresh water, such as brooks, springs, and fountains), river gods, and demons. The Greeks also worshiped demigods—beings who were half human and half god. One of the most famous of these was Alexander's reputed ancestor, Heracles (his Roman name was Hercules).

The God of Wine
The cult of Dyonisus (shown here in a fifth century B.C.E. painting) was popular among the Macedonians.

The cult of Dionysus was popular in Macedonia. The son of Zeus and a mortal woman, Dionysus was the god of nature and fertility and the giver of wine. Alexander's mother, Olympias, was a member of the cult of Dionysus and participated in rituals honoring him. She was said to have initiated Alexander into this cult at an early age. Alexander honored Dionysus at frequent drinking celebrations, known as *comuses*, and with dramatic performances.

The rules of behavior were based on what people believed the gods expected. For example, the Greeks believed the gods expected them to provide hospitality to strangers and proper burial for family members. They also believed the gods punished humans for arrogance and violence. When misfortune struck, it was considered a sign that someone had offended one of the gods. Offenses might include forgetting to make a sacrifice, violating the purity of a temple area, or breaking an oath or sworn agreement.

Indian Wise Men

When Alexander and his troops entered India in March 326 B.C.E., they met people who held a variety of faiths. At the time, Buddhism was about two centuries old and was spreading throughout India. The Buddha was an Indian prince who lived some time between 560 and 480 B.C.E. Saddened by the suffering of the world, he left his luxurious palace and spent the next six years meditating, after which he achieved enlightenment—the truth about the world and about the human condition. He taught that to live an unselfish life is the way to end suffering in the world. Some of Alexander's followers became Buddhists.

Alexander also encountered a group of Brahman sages, wise men who wandered naked without possessions and who were fed by the community. Having renounced (given up) all physical pleasures and the life of the flesh, they were detached from the joys and pains of the human condition.

Alexander, highly curious about Brahman beliefs, personally interviewed these sages. They told him that man experiences many lifetimes and that human existence is a punishment for previous mistakes. They also introduced him to the concept of nirvana, a mental state that enables people to escape from the never-ending chain of reincarnation, or being born again and again. Their religion was a forerunner of Hinduism.

When the holy men discovered that Alexander's goal was conquest, they stamped the ground to show him that you can only really possess the ground you stand on. Alexander disagreed, but admired their independence. One of them, Calanus (d. 324 B.C.E.), became his adviser and returned to Persia with Alexander.

The Greeks envisioned their gods as having human form and being, for the most part, physically perfect. Although they were all-powerful, they had many common human faults, and were capable of jealousy, revenge, pettiness, and vanity.

To appease the gods, people made sacrifices and offerings. Sacrifices were also made as thanks to the gods for blessings and to enlist their support. Alexander sacrificed to the gods before every battle as well as at many other times. The ritual of sacrifice was the primary form of contact between people and gods. While individuals could offer sacrifices in their homes, most sacrifices took place as regularly scheduled events on the community's civic calendar. Each city-state had a patron deity, or supporting god, and its citizens honored that god. Athens was named after Athena, the goddess of wisdom.

God or Man?

Greek mythology contains many stories of Zeus having children with human women. Many historians believe Oympias had told Alexander since his childhood that Zeus was his real father. When Alexander entered Egypt in 332 B.C.E., he visited the oasis of Siwa, home of a famous temple of the god Ammon, the Egyptian counterpart of Zeus. According to legend, the oracle confirmed that the god Ammon/Zeus was his true father.

Many historians dispute this story. One theory is that when Alexander entered the temple, the priest greeted him by calling him "my son," and that followers outside thought the words had been spoken by the god.

The secret of Siwa has never been known, because Alexander never told anyone what the oracle said to him. However, after that visit the king often wore two rams' horns—the sacred headdress of Ammon.

Later, Alexander petitioned Athens to ask that they grant him the status of god, which they reluctantly did.

Ritual offerings might include art, money and other valuables, fruits, vegetables, and small cakes. Animal sacrifice was a tradition that may have come from prehistoric hunters who wanted to show respect for the divine forces that provided them with animals for food. Animal sacrifice involved strict rules and elaborate procedures. Different cults had different rituals, all performed by priests and priestesses. One of the few rights Greek women had was that of becoming priestesses.

Every Greek temple was dedicated to a particular god, and these structures were looked upon as places where the deities they were built for actually lived. Temples were typically rectangular and constructed of marble. Inside stood brightly painted marble statues of the particular god or goddess, with an altar in front. Inside the temples there were special shrines known as oracles, at which the gods were believed to communicate with human beings. These communications, including answers to questions and interpretation of signs, came through a priest or priestess at the shrine, who was also called an oracle. Often the answers these oracles provided were not very clear and could have more than one meaning.

The Macedonians were very tolerant of other religions. For centuries, they had incorporated the beliefs and gods of other religions into their own, and Alexander offered sacrifices to the local gods in the areas he conquered.

Religions in the Persian Empire

Despite their autocratic rule, the kings of the Persian Empire allowed people in the nations they defeated to practice their own customs and follow their own religious beliefs. However, most people in the Persian Empire, along with the kings, followed Zoroastrianism. Its founder was a prophet named Zoroaster, whom historians believe to have lived some time between 1000 and 600 B.C.E. in what is now Uzbekistan. Zoroaster was the first of the great monotheistic prophets. (Monotheism is the belief that there is only one god.)

The Zoroastrians believe that there is one supreme god, Ahura-Mazda, and that he created everything that was good, including heaven, earth, people, truth, joy, light, and fire. But Ahura-Mazda had an evil twin brother, known simply as the Evil One, who created everything bad. In contrast to the Greeks, who believed that people's lives were controlled by the gods, the Persians believed they could choose between good or evil. Zoroaster preached that the world was the arena for a constant battle between good and evil. Every time someone did or thought something good, he or she was strengthening the power of Ahura-Mazda. Whenever people behaved badly, they were tipping the balance in favor of the Evil One.

Zoroaster discouraged animal sacrifice; he preached that animals were too valuable to kill. Fire

CONNECTIONS >>>>>>>>>>>>>

Gifts of the Magi

The leaders of Zoroastrianism were priests, or wise men, who were called *magi*. By the first century C.E. the word in its singular form—*magus* or *magos*—was often in use to mean a mysterious person who had access to secret knowledge that was not available to the common people. It also shows up in this kind of context in the Bible. From these roots came the word "magic."

The most famous magi were the three wise men who visited Jesus when he was born. A star is said to have led them to his location in a manger in Bethlehem. They brought him gifts of gold, frankincense, and myrrh—goods that were commonly traded between East and West.

CONNECTIONS >>>>>>>>>>>>>>>>>>>>>>>>>>>>>

Zoroastrianism Today

Zoroaster's teachings spread to nearby lands during the Hellenistic period, and influenced the development of other religions. For example, the Persians believed that Ahura-Mazda appointed a guardian angel for every person on earth. The concept of angels was later absorbed into the beliefs of Judaism and Christianity, along with other aspects of Zoroastrianism, such as a final judgment day.

Zoroastrian teachings have been passed down orally for centuries and its followers still perform ancient rituals, such as the lighting of lamps and tending of sacred trees. Fire still plays a central role, and Zoroastrian sanctuaries are called fire temples.

A modern Zoroastrian festival in Tehran.

In Iran today, Islam has largely replaced Zoroastrianism, but a few thousand Zoroastrians still practice their ancient religion there. The largest population of Iranian Zoroastrians can be found in the desert town of Yazd, which dates back to the Sassanian times (224–651 C.E.). Local Zoroastrians claim that the sacred fire housed inside Yazd's *ateshkadeh*, or fire temple, has been burning since the fourth century C.E.

Outside of Iran, the largest population of this religion can today be found in Bombay, India. Its members are descended from Persians who emigrated there more than a thousand years ago.

was an important part of Zoroastrian religious rituals, and many trees are considered to be sacred.

Unlike the Greeks, the peoples of the Persian Empire did not depict their gods as human beings. Stone carvings portrayed Ahura-Mazda as a winged deity who often appeared to be blessing the kings. Although people believed the Persian kings were superior to other humans, they were not considered gods but rather the agents of Ahura-Mazda.

Some people in the Persian Empire also worshiped other gods. For example, a popular religious festival in ancient Persia was held in honor of Mithra, the sun god.

CHAPTER 6

Art, Science, and Culture Across the Empire

AFTER ALEXANDER CONQUERED THE PERSIAN EMPIRE, Greek became the official language of government, education, and international commerce. Native languages continued to exist, most especially in Egypt, where Greek hardly permeated the country outside Alexandria. But all important discourse and documents were in Greek. A universal language enabled an unprecedented exchange of ideas. Education in the Greek language extended knowledge of Greek culture, and the Greeks and Macedonians also became increasingly aware of the achievements of other civilizations. Because of their high regard for knowledge and learning, they had many documents and books translated into Greek. As Eastern knowledge became more accessible to the West, new understanding began to challenge the old, clear-cut distinction between "civilized" Greeks and "barbarians."

Greek Ideals of Education

The power and lasting influence of the culture in which Alexander was raised, and which he spread, came from the Greek reverence for learning and for providing education with a philosophical basis. During Hellenism, education became more widespread in both Greece and the former Persian Empire, but in both societies it was exclusively available to the wealthy and, for the most part, only to boys.

Among the poor, the level of literacy in Greece was very low. Most poor people could do little more than sign their names. It was easy, however, for most people to find someone who could read to them if they needed to understand a written text, such as a letter. Most communication was therefore oral rather than written. This meant most people were

Influential Style
A leaping ram decorates this bronze oil lamp, found in Shabwah, in modern-day. Yemen. Its sophisticated style is Hellenistic.

able to absorb a lot of information by ear. Even those who could read usually read out loud. Both rich and poor Greeks liked songs, speeches, and stories, and memorized many of them. In Persia, too, most people were illiterate, and recited stories and poems from memory.

In contrast, male children of wealthy Greek parents were highly educated. That education was aimed at the complete individual, as Greeks had little respect for specialists, not even great athletes or philosophers. Their ideal man was someone who was both a philosopher and an athlete, who could take part intelligently in public affairs and also fight well. He would also have to be a witty guest at a party or banquet, since lively conversation was highly valued.

The Greeks believed that a healthy body was necessary for a good mind. Boys attended different schools for mental and physical training. Wealthier families might hire a private tutor or have a household slave, called a pedagogue, teach children at home.

Greek boys from well-to-do families started going to school when they were seven years old. Until the age of 14, they focused on reading, writing, numbers, and music. They learned to read by studying Homer's two great works, The Iliad and The Odyssey. To practice writing, they used a sharp wooden stick, called a *stylus*, to write on a waxed wooden block that could be scraped clean and used again and again. When the wax wore down to the wood, they simply applied more wax. Boys learned numbers using pebbles and an abacus, or counting board. Students who misbehaved in class were struck with a rod.

In music school, boys learned to play pipes as well as the flute and the lyre, a stringed instrument with a sound box made from the shell of a tortoise. The strings were plucked with a disk called a plectrum (a word we still use in English). At almost every Greek social event, music was played.

Great Teacher

Aristotle teaches Alexander in this 17th century European drawing. Aristotle was considered one of the greatest scholars and philosophers of his day, and is still widely admired.

When boys reached the age of 14, other subjects were added to their curriculum. These included geometry, literature, astronomy, drawing, rhetoric (the art of discourse and speechmaking, communication, and interpretation), and sports. Sports took place in a gymnasium, where boys exercised naked. The main sport was wrestling. The goal of a wrestling match was to force the opponent's shoulders to the ground three times. Boys were also taught to dance.

Higher education began in the fourth century B.C.E. in Athens, at the academy founded by the philosopher Plato (427–347 B.C.E.). Schools of philosophy were available for men over 18. These provided more or less a college education. The leading philosopher of the school would deliver lectures, conduct panel discussions, and pose questions to the students.

Alexander's Education

As a Macedonian prince being groomed for the throne, Alexander received a first-rate education. But he did not always enjoy his educational experiences. His first tutor was a man named Leonidas. The stern Leonidas toughened Alexander physically. The young student was required by his teacher to engage in physical exercise before dawn and sometimes had to march for hours before breakfast to increase his appetite. Leonidas insisted on a lean, simple diet and believed being hungry was good discipline. He would search Alexander's belongings to make sure his mother, Olympias, had not snuck him any treats.

Leonidas taught Alexander skills such as running, memorizing lessons, riding a horse bareback, driving a chariot, and using a sword and a spear. Historians have credited Alexander's later ability to endure the many extreme hardships of his war campaigns to the tough discipline he was subjected to under Leonidas's tutelage.

When Alexander was 13, his father hired Plato's student, Aristotle, to replace Leonidas. With this great teacher Alexander studied literature, philosophy, ethics, metaphysics, geography, zoology, botany, scientific criticism, drama, poetry, art, law, and politics. Both physical and spiritual qualities were emphasized in the young prince's education. He learned to sing and play a lyre and received training in physical fitness and warfare. Aristotle also instilled in his young student a lifelong love of the writings of Homer. Alexander believed in the Homeric concept of personal success for the sake of honor and glory, and tried to emulate his heroes Heracles and Achilles.

Alexander had a great respect for learning, and during his years in the Middle East he often ordered books to be sent to him from Greece. He

THE ART OF RHETORIC

Rhetoric and oratory were important aspects of a Greek education. Oratory is the art of speaking well in public. Rhetoric is the skill of marshalling arguments that inspire and persuade. A person might have one skill and lack the other. The truly accomplished person, such as Alexander, had both. His career is punctuated by a series of rousing speeches that inspired his soldiers when the odds were against them.

Perhaps Alexander's most famous speech is the one he gave at Opis about a year before his death. He spoke of his vision for a united empire, and prevented his army from mutinying. Known as the Oath of Alexander, the speech urged people to live in peace as one nation, without distinguishing between Greeks and "barbarians." Although many people have pointed to the Oath of Alexander as an inspiring call for peace and world unity, many historians doubt the authenticity of any versions of the speech that are today circulated.

Hot baths first became widespread in Greece in the fourth century B.C.E., so they would have been a luxury Alexander enjoyed. Greek men took as many as three or four baths in a day, and Alexander took several baths a day throughout his life—mostly in rivers.

Most bathtubs were in public bathhouses, but the wealthy also had bathing facilities at home. Attendants helped bathers by pouring water over their bodies. The bath was not only a means of washing. It was the medium of divine purification, a spiritual event. It was thought to renew the soul.

Baths were also considered necessary for the health of the human body. A complete body bath was prescribed for healing hysteria. Soaking the head in cold water was prescribed for a hemorrhage, or massive bleeding. Sponge baths were a means to calm and relax. Such healing baths had very specific rules and required skilled assistants, a room with fresh air, and specific sacrifices.

also sent Aristotle a great deal of money over the years to fund his research and educational projects.

In some cases, the king also looked after the education of his troops' children. As the army moved from place to place, many soldiers left behind children who were half Persian and half Greek or Macedonian. Alexander made many of these children wards of the state and arranged for their education. They were given military instruction and also learned about the ideals of Greek culture.

"Modern Medicine" in Alexander's Time

Medicine in ancient Greece dates back thousands of years, but the first real hospitals there came into being, according to historians, in the fourth century B.C.E., the time of Alexander. Greek knowledge and techniques of health and healing were already so well-known and respected by then that Romans often employed Greek physicians rather that Roman ones, who were usually slaves. Ancient Greek writings indicate that even the peoples of the Persian Empire preferred Greek, and sometimes Egyptian, doctors.

In Alexander's day, herbs had become an important part of the healing arts. Myrrh, frankincense, and many other herbs were used in the treatment of disease, though no one really understood why they worked. Garlic was used as a remedy for, among other things, breathing ailments, parasites, and insomnia. Baths were important for purification of body and soul.

Also in Alexander's time, Asclepius healing cults were commonplace, with many active healing temples throughout Greece. One of the most common practices in these temples was incubation—a technique of healing that involved sleeping through the night wrapped in a white sheet and hoping for remedies or cures to be provided in dreams. Ill patients came from all over in hopes of being healed through incubation. Ancient records attest to many apparently miraculous cures, after which the happy patient would leave some form of payment at the temple. The poorest left whatever they could—a lock of hair, their shoes, or simply sang a song of gratitude. Wealthier patients paid accordingly.

Eastern and Western Science

Science blossomed during the Hellenistic age. Because of the increase in the exchange of ideas between East and West, rapid progress was made in a number of fields, including philosophy, medicine, mathematics, and others. Greek and Babylonian scholars collaborated in the areas of mathematics, science, and astronomy. Technology also advanced, and many new machines and instruments were invented.

As in other areas, much more is known about Greek science than about science in the Persian Empire. One reason is that an impressive Greek collection of literary, scientific, and other texts still exists, while documents predating Alexander's conquests have not fared as well. This is partly because as papyrus became more commonly used, clay tablets were forgotten. But papyrus was hard to preserve in climates other than that of Egypt. Therefore, beyond several relatively short public inscriptions, there is little written documentation of the period between the fall of Nineveh in Assyria in 612 B.C.E. and Alexander's invasion—a fact that has long frustrated scholars and historians. One thing that *is* clear is that the scientific perspectives of Greece and the Middle East were very different. The Greeks believed everything could be understood through science, that knowledge was based on reason, and that all the natural sciences rested on a foundation of mathematics and geometry. This rationalism, which advocated mastery of a subject through the method of inquiry, even challenged the Greeks' traditional religious beliefs. Today, mathematics and rationalism still underlie the Western approach to science.

The Greeks were the first to develop many fields of science and they furthered most of those already in existence. Scientists included practitioners of philosophy, geometry, physics, economics, mathematics, chemistry, biology, psychology, and other fields.

In the Persian Empire people also studied, explored, and experimented, but they did not share the Greeks' approach to science. For them, there was no separation between science and religion; science was an outgrowth of the divine. They did not want to master the world through scientific knowledge, but instead wished to learn how to adapt to the forces that affected the world. Their science was based on personal experience, not on analysis, theory, and methodology. Nevertheless, they made many contributions to the world of science.

Ancient Star Gazing

The city of Babylon, in central Mesopotamia, was a center of science and mathematics. Babylonian mathematicians made great advances in geometry and were among the greatest astronomers in the world. They calculated the distance of the sun and the moon from the earth with great precision. They understood scientific facts that would not be widely known elsewhere until Galileo's discoveries in the early 17h century. They knew, for example, that

the earth turned on its axis, that planets revolve around the sun, and that the sun is much larger than the earth.

Each night for centuries, Babylonian astronomers and priests climbed to the tops of tall towers to observe the moon and stars and record their movements. They kept track of celestial phenomena, such as the exact times the sun and moon rose and set.

One of the discoveries Alexander's men made in Babylon was the astronomical diary of the temple of Marduk, the most important Babylonian god. The officials of this sanctuary had systematically described their celestial observations. One of them, Kidinnu, was the first to accurately estimate the length of the year. He calculated that a year was 365 days, 5 hours, 44 minutes, 12.52 seconds (instead of 48 minutes, 45.17 seconds, which was generally accepted at the time), and proposed a reform of the calendar based on these findings.

When the reports of the Babylonian astronomers were translated into Greek, this new knowledge was immediately applied. The Greek astronomer Callippus (c. 370–c. 300 B.C.E.) recalculated the lunar month and came up with a new calendar that had a slightly longer cycle than the Greeks had previously used. His new era began on June 28, 330 B.C.E.—only eight months after Alexander captured Babylon.

Middle Eastern astronomers also discovered that there were two days each year, one in the spring and one in the fall, when night and day are of equal lengths. These days are now called equinoxes, which means "equal nights."

Reading the Signs

Personal horoscopes were first developed in Babylon about 50 years before Alexander was born. A horoscope is a chart based on the position of the sun, moon, and planets at the time of a baby's birth. The ancient astronomers believed that people's personalities and actions were determined or influenced by the position of the heavens when they were born. It was common for ancient people to make important decisions based on their horoscopes. Many people throughout the world still believe in this practice,

What Is Your Sign?
Personal horoscopes were developed in Babylon about 50 years before Alexander was born, and have been popular ever since. This zodiac (c. 1550) appears in an Italian manuscript and shows the Atlantic Hemisphere in the center.

known as astrology. In some eastern countries, astrology is considered a science. In the West, while many people believe in astrology, it is not generally thought of as a science.

Interpreting celestial phenomena was one of many ways ancient people believed they could divine, or predict, the future. Another form of divination involved birds. Bird observers were common in Asia Minor, and predicted the future based on the behavior of birds, particularly fighting birds.

In Greece, predicting the future was also considered an important scientific pursuit. Divination involved various methods of understanding what the gods were communicating to humans. Ancient Greeks used dreams to make predictions and to provide clues as to what humans might have done to anger the gods. They depended on soothsayers, also known as seers, divinators, or prophets, to interpret signs and omens. The Greeks widely trusted these seers to accurately understand and interpret omens such as the weather, the flight of birds, and other phenomena that they believed revealed what the gods were thinking or planning.

One of Alexander's most valued advisors was the seer Aristander. Whenever something important was planned, or any time something strange happened or a new phenomenon was encountered, Aristander's job was to interpret its meaning.

Before battles, Alexander sacrificed animals to the gods to enlist their support for the Macedonians. Marks on the animal's entrails

Signs and Omens

It is said that on the night Alexander cut the Gordian knot (see page 20), a violent storm came up and the skies shook with thunder and lightning. Seers interpreted the storm as a sign that Zeus was pleased with Alexander's accomplishment and would give his armies victory.

One of the most famous predictions concerns the founding of Alexandria in Egypt. Alexander poured peeled barley to mark out a plan for streets and the locations where he wanted certain buildings to be placed. Birds ate the barley, which Alexander at first saw as a bad omen. However, Aristander said it meant the city would attract a great number of settlers and that they would all be provided with sustenance.

After Alexander's murder of his friend Cleitus in a drunken rage (see page 41), soothsayers found omens that they believed had predicted this event. For one, when Cleitus entered the banquet hall, some sheep followed him in, which was later interpreted as a sign that the gods had intended him to become a sacrifice.

In the spring of 328 B.C.E., soldiers discovered two springs welling out of the ground by the side of the Oxus River, where the army had set up camp. One was water, the other was a liquid that the soldiers compared to olive oil. No one realized at the time that it was petroleum, the oily, flammable substance used today in making gasoline and other products. When Aristander was called on to interpret this omen, he said the spring was a sign that there would be hard labors ahead, followed by victory.

(internal organs) were believed to be omens that indicated how the battle would turn out. Special hooks were used to pull the flesh back from the organs so the marks could be revealed. Before the decisive Battle of Gaugamela, for example, Aristander predicted victory based on his examination of the entrails of a ram that had been sacrificed. This sign agreed with another omen—an eclipse of the moon that occurred shortly before the battle, which Aristander had interpreted to mean that the Macedonians would win at Gaugamela.

Military strategies were often based on the interpretation of omens. When an eagle landed on a rock near ships on the Phoenician coast, Aristander saw this as an omen that Alexander should look for victory on land instead of at sea. This proved to be a successful strategy.

Throughout Alexander's campaigns, favorable omens gave him confidence that the gods were blessing his endeavors. But not all omens were encouraging. Some accounts of Alexander's final entrance into Babylon, in 323 B.C.E., mention that a large number of ravens filled the skies. The birds were pecking each other and some fell dead at the feet of the returning king. Soothsayers, believing this to be a bad omen, advised him not to enter the city. Astronomers cautioned him that the stars also foretold trouble if he went ahead. Alexander did not heed their warnings. Instead, he marched triumphantly into the city. A few months later, in Babylon, he died.

Ancient Technologies

It is difficult to determine what Greek technologies Alexander may have introduced into the East, but during his time many practical methods of gathering information and making life simpler were in use. Mapmaking was one of these methods. At a time when few people knew much about the world beyond their own town or farm, mapmaking, though difficult, was a crucial activity. One method used by the mapmakers who traveled with Alexander was to count and record the number of steps they took each day walking from one camp to the next. Their footstep counts were used as the basis for the maps they created.

The science of metrology (the theory and investigation of making measurements) in Alexander's time is not well documented. One thing that is known is that Alexander's conquests had significant impact on the development of this science in the lands he controlled. These regions widely adopted the Greek metrological systems, and the widespread minting of coins under Alexander's rule made it practical to give the various coins

FLOATING BRIDGES

Alexander's soldiers built floating bridges across Indian rivers. They did this by lashing boats together and putting planks of wood on top of them. They could then porter supplies and horses across them. This method of building bridges is still used in the Punjab.

names for the first time. The names corresponded to their given monetary value, making it easier to standardize the relative value of goods.

The peoples of the former Persian Empire made innovations of their own during this time. They developed an ingenious method of dispatching royal orders across their vast empire. Between Susa and Persepolis, they placed high lookout posts close enough for a shout to be heard between them. The local inhabitants with the loudest voices were stationed at these posts as guards. A guard would pass along an order by shouting it across to the next guard, who would do the same until the message had been delivered. In this way, an order traveling the distance of a 30-day journey by foot would be received on the same day.

Another essential technology helped move water from one place to another. Because of the arid climate in which they lived, the people in the Middle East had a great respect for water, which led to the development of a system for transporting water throughout their empire, known as *qanats*. *Qanats* were underground channels that carried water from the foothills of the mountains in the north to remote, dry areas, such as the plains regions of the south. This irrigation system linked many wells along its route. The

CONNECTIONS >>>>>>>>>>>>>>>>>>>>>>>>>>>>>>>>>

Darius Was Here

Persia's system of *qanats*, introduced in about 500 B.C.E., was crucial for carrying water to remote places of that arid eastern empire. As recently as 1933, all of the city of Tehran's water came from this underground irrigation system. One *qanat* linked the Nile River to the Red Sea. Along the length of this great *qanat*, which was 87 miles long and 164 feet wide, were a number of monuments.

In the 1860s, when workers were digging the Suez Canal (which connects the Mediterranean Sea with the Red Sea), they found fragments of a red granite monument marking Darius' *qanat* that had at one time stood about 9.8 feet tall and 8.2 feet wide. It bore an inscription written in four languages, including Old Persian, Babylonian, Elamite (the language of Elam, an ancient kingdom in today's southwestern Iran) and Egyptian. According to A.T. Olmstead's book *History of the Persian Empire*, the words, from Darius I, read, "I am a Persian. From Parsa I seized Egypt. I commanded this canal to be dug from the river, Nile by name, which flows in Egypt, to the sea which goes From Parsa. Afterward this canal was dug as I commanded, and ships passed from Egypt through this canal to Parsa as was my command."

qanat tunnels reached down and into the water table. Other shafts provided ventilation and access for cleaning and repairing the tunnels. This technology spread because of a policy King Darius I had introduced: As an incentive to people to spend the time and money to build *qanats*, he decreed that anyone who conveyed water to dry areas would be allowed to cultivate the land for five generations.

Gardens of Paradise

The Persian reverence for clean water and good soil was rooted in the people's love of farming and gardening. They enjoyed all flowers, especially those with rich, heavy fragrances, but they revered the rose above all others. Sacred ancient Persian texts speak of roses as first being cultivated by angels.

The Rose of Damascus, one of the most fragrant species and a flower with a long history, grew wild in the Middle East. Gardeners often transplanted it from the wilds into their gardens, along with other wild flowers. This exotic rose eventually found its way to Spain with the Moors and to France with the Crusaders, and it became known in England during the time of Henry the VIII (1491–1547). In the Western world the Rose of Damascus became known as the much-loved Damask Rose.

Alexander's admiration for the gardens he saw in the Persian Empire deeply influenced the design of Hellenistic and, later, Roman gardens. His experience of the palaces and gardens of the East, accompanied by his governors who later became his successors, also had a great influence on the entire design of the city of Alexandria.

Hellenistic Art

Along with science, the arts also flourished in the Hellenistic world, especially painting, sculpture, crafts, and architecture. Greek designs became more complicated as a result of the influence of ideas and techniques from other lands. Similarly, artists in Asia and the Middle East adopted elements of the Greek style. The commingling of these two approaches evolved into a new style of art that incorporated both Greek and Asian design.

This new style became known as Hellenistic art and was characterized by a greater sense of naturalism, especially in portraying the human body, than was found in earlier works. Hellenistic art also reflected a move from religious themes to a focus on more intense human emotions and psychologically oriented portrayals of its subject matter. Often Hellenistic art features more dramatic poses and high contrasts between light and shadow as well.

FATHER OF BOTANY

The philosopher Theophrastus (c. 372–c. 287 B.C.E.) is sometimes called the father of botany, which is the study of plants. He gave botany its start by writing detailed books about plant life, such as his *Historia Plantarum*. Much of the information in Theophrastus's writings was said to have been gathered by Alexander during his eastern campaigns.

Greek artists first began to portray the human form in this new way during the fifth century B.C.E. During the classical age of Greece (approximately 500 to 400 B.C.E.), sculptors and other artists experimented with new techniques and approaches. While the paintings and sculptures of earlier civilizations were often stiff and not lifelike, the Greeks became the first to model realistic human forms in their art. Though no Greek paintings have survived, much sculpture remains, most of it made of marble or bronze.

The influence of Greek art can be traced all along Alexander's path, from the Hindu Kush Mountains to the mouth of the Indus River. Archaeologists have discovered many buildings and statues on the border of India and Persia that show the influence of Greek art. These works are naturalistic and sophisticated—much more so than the art that predated Alexander's arrival. In the region of Gandhara in India (which corresponds today with the countries of Afghanistan and Pakistan), which Alexander invaded in 326 B.C.E., a new style of art was developed that integrated Buddhist thought with Greek artistic

concepts. The Gandhara style played an important role in the development of Indian art; for example, many statues of the Buddha were modeled after the Greek god Apollo. Even in Turkestan and China, countries Alexander never visited, the Buddha statues are influenced by Greek sculptural style. Early Christian art was Hellenistic as well.

Alexander's long march through many different regions, often with skilled craftsmen attached to his army, enabled artisans from many regions to share their skills, or at least see each other's work. Greek craftsmen, who were considered among the best in the world, were influenced by Persian crafts. For example, they became familiar with the Persian rhyton, an ornate drinking vessel often made in the shape of an animal's head. After the war, large quantities of such rhytons appeared in Athens, where Greek artists immediately began imitating them.

Blending Styles

The Gandhara style of art in India combined Buddhist thought with Greek artistic ideals. This stucco Indian head of a Bodhisattva (goddess), dating from about the 4th century C.E., clearly shows the Greek sculptural style in its natural representation of the face.

Not all Hellenistic artworks were of high quality. Many local artists did not know how to apply the principles of Greek art, and the emphasis in some areas was on quantity rather than quality. More works of art were produced than ever before, but many were pretentious and few were masterpieces.

Some art critics believe that one such overwrought work, called by some a "monstrosity," was the Colossus of Rhodes. But many ancients hailed its great beauty. The Colossus, a towering male figure erected to watch over the harbor of the Mediterranean island of Rhodes in Greece, was one of the so-called Seven Wonders of the Ancient World. At 110 feet tall, it was so huge that a grown man would not have been able to wrap his arms around a single finger of the figure. The Colossus was destroyed in an earthquake in about 225 B.C.E., so its true artistic worth will never be known. But one fact is known: It inspired the French sculptor Auguste Bartholdi (1834–1904). Based on what he imagined the Colossus of Rhodes looked like, he created America's Statue of Liberty, which stands at the same height, also watching over a great city at the edge of the water.

Architecture

Perhaps nowhere was the Greek influence more obvious than in city planning and architecture. This was not only true in the new towns that Alexander founded but also in existing cities. Virtually everywhere that Alexander's conquests took him, Greek and Macedonian soldiers settled. Some—those injured or too old—were regularly left behind as the troops pressed onward. Others, once their army service was done, returned to places within the new kingdom that they had earlier marched through or fought in. When they settled, they brought with them the Greek vision of what a good metropolis should be. The locations of streets and buildings were planned according to Greek standards and the design of new buildings was based on Greek ideals of architecture.

According to the Greek model, public structures were needed for political, economic, and recreational activities. As Alexander conquered and founded cities and his soldiers settled in them, huge building projects became commonplace. Government facilities, public meeting houses, courts of law, and gymnasia sprung up alongside Macedonian-style palaces and the religious and military facilities that were an equally important part of everyday life. Everywhere could be seen Greek style homes adorned with Greek terra cottas and pottery as well as other forms of Greek decoration and domestic items.

The Macedonians also built stadiums, hippodromes (oval stadiums for chariot races), theaters, and amphitheaters. They created colonnaded streets and public baths. These structures lasted until the Arab invasions, and even then two of them—the *agora*, or market, and the *balaneia* or *thermae*, the baths—were not wiped out but preserved to become an important part of Islamic culture as well.

Ornate Persian Design

Persian design was more colorful, grandiose, and intricate than that of Greece. The kings of the Persian Empire built magnificent palaces and decorated them lavishly. The stairway of King Darius's palace at Persepolis was carved with portraits of people from many different parts of his empire. The vast royal hall, supported by many dozens of carved stone columns, could hold 10,000 people. Artisans from across the empire carved numerous stone monuments in Persepolis and other royal capitals.

Stone carvings often portrayed the kings' pride in their military conquests. Monuments carved on cliffs depicted great military achievements, showing victorious leaders and defeated enemies.

Unlike Persepolis, Susa was not close to sources of stone. The construction of the royal palace at Susa depended on materials brought in from throughout the empire, including wood, gold, silver, ebony, and ivory. The palace also incorporated styles and techniques from craftsmen from the far reaches of the empire, including stonecutters, goldsmiths, woodworkers, and glazed-brick makers. It was decorated with pictures of men, monsters, and gods made from tiles and glazed bricks. The clay bricks were coated with colorful glazes made of crushed rocks, salt, and powdered clay and baked in a kiln (a large, very hot oven) to create a thin, shiny surface.

Babylon was a spectacular city, with a huge temple and a great royal palace. The road leading to the temple was decorated with lions, flowers, and patterns made of glazed bricks. The palace's hanging gardens were famous throughout the ancient world (see page 32).

From the wealth of materials that came into their empire, the people of the Persian Empire created all kinds of beautiful works. They made fine jewelry out of silver and carpets out of wool. These intricately designed carpets were highly valued and are still very expensive and rare today. Persian nobles decorated their homes with beautiful sculptures, delicate vases, and luxurious fabrics. Their homes, like the palaces, were designed to command respect.

Unlike building design in the East during Alexander's time, Greek architecture was typically very regular and rectangular in shape. But a

SEVEN WONDERS OF THE ANCIENT WORLD

The Seven Wonders of the Ancient World were the major landmarks of the Hellenistic world. The first three were the statue of Zeus in Olympia, the Great Pyramids in Egypt, and the hanging gardens of Babylon. These three sites form a triangle that identifies the economic heartland of the Hellenistic civilization.

The other four wonders were the Temple of Artemis in Ephesos, the Mausoleum in Halicarnassus, the Colossus of Rhodes, and the Pharos, or lighthouse, of Alexandria. Of all these wonders, only the Great Pyramids remain today.

number of round buildings were constructed as well. These exceptions, which include *tholoi*—circular buildings with pointed or domed roofs—are considered by some to be a result of the Persian influence on Greek architecture.

There was another important result of this fusion of West and East. The great stores of wealth that Alexander laid claim to in the Persian Empire had a direct and striking effect on architecture and building in Greece, as well as in the conquered lands. Before Alexander's time, even traditional Greek buildings such as gymnasia and theaters had been relatively primitive. With the riches that Alexander and his army poured back into circulation, such buildings became monumental complexes of the finest order. The sometimes awe-inspiring appearance of Greek architecture that today we take for granted as "how it was done" in Greece could not have been possible without Alexander's eastern expansion.

Recreation and Leisure

The Greeks gave as much importance to buildings for entertainment and leisure activities as they did their architecture for business and political purposes, and Alexander's contemporaries, like the king himself, were great fans of entertainment of all kinds.

Among the favorite activities of Greek men were good conversation, athletics, and politics. In the afternoon, men would attend a lecture, exercise at a gymnasium, or bathe in a public bathhouse. Relaxing at the public baths was a primary form of recreation. Some of the baths contained gambling rooms where men would throw dice or play a game called knucklebones, or five-stones, which was similar to jacks.

Dinner parties were also a favorite leisure activity of the Macedonians and the Greeks. Following dinner, wealthy men often held a symposium, or drinking party. At these all-male festivities, guests would engage in intellectual discussions about political or scientific topics, taking turns to speak. They would also pose riddles to one another. A guest who was unable to solve the riddle would have to drink a glass of salted wine as punishment. Acrobats, singers, musicians, and dancers entertained at these gatherings, and there were few events that did not include music.

Younger Greeks had their own forms of amusement as well. Like their elders, teenagers played knucklebones, a game similar to dice that is still popular in some places today. Players throw and catch five small objects, originally sheep's knucklebones, in different ways. Teens also played with balls and tops, and played hopscotch and a game that is similar to marbles but which used nuts instead.

Board games were another popular entertainment, mostly among adults. Many of these boards featured a circular path that had to be traversed to win. The Greeks invented a feature that is still a common part of many board games today—the path with squares containing messages of reward or punishment coming to any player who lands there.

Persians enjoyed singing songs, storytelling, and reciting poetry. They played a variety of musical instruments, including harps, flutes, and tambourines.

Games and Festivals

Alexander carried the Greek tradition of elaborate, well-attended events with him as he moved relentlessly east. One of the most important ways the Greeks honored their gods was by holding various public festivals, and the Greek calendar is filled with religious and civic contests and games. Athens had the largest number of religious festivals in Greece, with nearly half the days of the year featuring a large or small festival.

Not everyone attended all the festivals. The contracts of hired laborers spelled out exactly which religious ceremonies they could attend. Married women had their own festival, a three-day celebration in honor of the goddess Demeter.

Some festivals honored gods not only with sacrifices and parades, but also with contests in music, dancing, poetry, and athletics. Valuable prizes were awarded to the winners. Funeral games honored a dead warrior by reenacting his military skills. The most famous contests were the Olympic Games, held in the city of Olympia every four years during the summer.

Athletes in Alexander's time, all male, competed in the nude. Slaves, foreigners, and convicts were barred from entering the games as competitors and women were not allowed to watch the games at all. Winners were celebrated and received cash, free meals for the rest of their lives, exemption from taxes, and other benefits.

Alexander and his men held festivals and tournaments wherever the army stopped for a time. For large festivals, they would create a city of tents for the actors, poets, singers, and musicians they brought in from Greece. They set up banners on gilded poles, held gymnastic and literary competitions, and organized foot and chariot races.

Epilogue

FROM THE WESTERN EDGES OF THE ONCE-IMPRESSIVE Persian Empire to the remote reaches of India and Pakistan, scratch the surface of modern life–travel away from the cosmopolitan, urban centers or speak to those whose ancestry dates back centuries in the same area– and traces of Alexander the Great are still easy to find. His influence shows up in the language, art, and current customs of many lands once claimed by him. The name of Alexander is still spoken in countless tales, both heroic and horrifying. In every way, the far-reaching impact of Alexander's conquests still resounds today.

One of the most profound aspects of this impact was in bringing the Greek language and customs into the areas under his dominion. By this single act he set the stage for the rapid exchange of knowledge and ideas over thousands of miles and throughout many formerly disparate cultural groups. Ultimately, the unity created by having one language so widely spoken dramatically altered the evolution of world culture. People who before could never have communicated with one another could now join in the flow of current thought and commerce.

Tales of Triumph and Terror

Traces of Alexander are found not only in the names associated with the many places he claimed for himself. From the mountains of the Hindu Kush to the capital of Egypt to the eastern shores of the Mediterranean and even beyond, reminders of Alexander's existence can still be detected. He is found in preserved art and crumbling architecture, and in old coins exchanged in rural markets that seem straight out of the 2,000-year-old past. And of course, he is enshrined as the central figure in hundreds of stories.

OPPOSITE
Still an Inspiration
The 2004 movie Alexander was written and directed by Oliver Stone and starred Colin Farrell (pictured) as Alexander, Angelina Jolie as his mother, Val Kilmer as Philip, Rosario Dawson as Roxane, and Jared Leto as Hephaestion.

Just inland from the eastern Mediterranean coast stand the massive ruins of Apollo's temple of Didyma, where Alexander stopped early in his eastward campaign. Legend has it that the sacred spring there had dried up since the Persians looted and desecrated the temple in 494 B.C.E. But upon Alexander's arrival to pay homage to Apollo, they say, the spring suddenly began to flow again. Soon after, according to the ancient writings, the new priestess of the temple foretold King Darius's death and Alexander's triumph in the East.

The whole of Alexander's journey is marked with spots like this. The so-called Wall of Alexander, a fortress wall built at the northern edge of today's Iran by Parthian kings after Alexander's death, stretches east from the Caspian Sea for 124 miles. In Herat, Afghanistan, the rough-looking mud brick remains of an old fort mark the area where he founded his city of Alexandria in Areia. In Kandahar, Afghanistan, archaeologists discovered a temple portraying Alexander as a god, with inscriptions in Greek and the biblical language of Aramaic. In 1939, a huge treasure was found north of Kabul, at the foot of the Hindu Kush Mountains where Alexander had a base. When the remains of this Hellenistic city were unearthed, among other riches archaeologists retrieved Alexandrian glass, ivory sculptures from India, and lacquered objects from China, all testifying to the trade that began blossoming under Alexander's rule.

All this is just a small fraction of the physical evidence that remains in the 21st century, and on four continents, of a ruthlessly ambitious conqueror. But Alexander's life, and his powerful and contradictory personality, comes most alive in the hundreds of stories that have been preserved and passed down—and probably fantastically elaborated upon over the centuries as well.

In particular, the stories, plays, and songs that portray him in his most demonic persona—that of the Great Iskander, the destroying, two-horned beast—seem to be most vividly expressed. The tales of Alexander's evil exploits are gleefully relayed in dusty roadside *caravanserai*, or inns. They are danced to by campfires in ancient mountains and listened to wide-eyed in the darkened bedrooms of modern-day Middle Eastern children. He even shows up in Muslim Shiite folk plays, where his attire often includes jodhpurs (English-style riding breeches) and a pith helmet.

The tales of Alexander's life and deeds, which range from reasonably believable to laughably impossible, are not confined to the lands that he conquered, either. He stars in legends and romances originating in places as far away as Western Europe, China, and Ethiopia, where, in some works,

Alexander's father, King Philip, is portrayed as a Christian martyr and Alexander himself as a holy religious saint.

He has also made a name for himself in Hollywood. In 1955, actor Richard Burton starred in the film *Alexander the Great,* and in the fall of 2004 he was reincarnated again. This time audiences saw him do heroic battle in the Oliver Stone movie *Alexander.*

One common story told throughout Asia even today is also depicted on old sculptures in some European cathedrals. It tells of Alexander as the two-horned monster who takes over the entire world. Then, still seething with ambition, he plots a god-like chariot ride into the heavens. His destruction comes when God casts him down for being consumed by hubris, or hugely self-satisfied pride.

In the telling of these tales over time, Alexander has taken on mythical proportions in the imaginations of so many who have heard them. Like any hero or monster worth remembering, he is larger than life, coming through the centuries to us as indelibly furious, ferocious, and wondrous.

Macedonia Today

The story of Macedonia's history after the death of Alexander is, like Alexander himself, neither simple nor peaceful. When Alexander's successor in Macedonia, Cassander, seized the throne, it led to civil war and almost continual chaos and political upheaval for nearly the next 50 years. In 276 B.C.E., Antigonus II (320–239 B.C.E.) became king of Macedonia, finally bringing some stability to the country and starting a dynasty that lasted until 168 B.C.E

During the second and third centuries B.C.E., Macedonia went to war with Rome four times, the last three with disastrous results. At the end of the fourth war, which lasted from 149 to 148 B.C.E., Macedonia was made a province of a Roman state that was just at the beginning of its rise to vast power.

Because of its unique geographical position as a crossroads between East and West, Macedonia has historically been a coveted possession for invaders coming from every direction. It was considered a crucial holding during the Byzantine Empire, and near the end of the 14th century it was absorbed into the large territory ruled by the Turkish Ottoman Empire. Macedonia remained relatively stable under this influence until 1912, when the Turks were finally pushed out of Europe by an alliance between Greece, Serbia, Montenegro, and Bulgaria. This conflict became known as the first Balkan War.

THE LAST GREEK

In the 1930s archaeologists excavated a huge tower close to Persepolis and facing the Naqsh-e Rustam tombs of the Achaemenian kings. On the tower were writings in Greek, Parthian, and Middle Persian, which described the successful wars against Rome waged by Persian king Shapur I (d. 272 C.E.) in the third century. Historians consider this a significant record because it was the last time the Greek language appeared in any Iranian inscription.

A Source of Pride
The Macedonian flag is carried by protesters as they march through Skopje in 2001. Macedonians staged the protest march after 10 Macedonian soldiers were killed in an ambush by ethnic Albanian rebels. Political and ethnic conflicts continue to plague the region.

But more than 500 years of Islamic rule had had a profound effect on every aspect of Macedonia's culture. Everything from religion to politics to daily customs of eating and dress were influenced by the Turks. The multifaceted mix of different ethnicities and cultural traditions further complicated the Macedonian national identity.

When the victors in the Balkan Wars divided up the lands they had wrested from the Turks, the territory that Alexander the Great had once called home was split into three parts. The southern portion, Greek Macedonia, became a part of Greece. This Macedonia is still located in the region of northern Greece where Alexander lived and became king, but it is smaller than it was in his time.

The northern portion, except for a small territory given to Bulgaria, went to Serbia. After World War I a new kingdom was formed made up of Serbian Macedonia, Croatia, and Slovenia. This became the country of Yugoslavia in 1929. In the following years, this northern Macedonia was constantly subjected to manipulation by outsiders trying to impose their own various visions of what the country should be. Finally in 1991, as Yugoslavia was breaking apart, the country declared its independence, keeping the name of Macedonia. The complexities of this and the difficulties that arise from the country's intricate ethnic mix caused and continue to cause much confusion, chaos, and international concern in the modern world.

Believing that by calling itself Macedonia the new republic was making an attempt to lay claim to Greek Macedonia, Greece loudly objected. Under this pressure from Greece, the new republic modified its name to the Former Yugoslav Republic of Macedonia, now simply known as the Republic of Macedonia. Additionally, the newly independent country agreed to redesign its flag–which had featured the ancient Greek symbol known as the Star of Vergina.

These days the people of the Republic of Macedonia are, for the most part, of Slavic descent. But for many, their connections to Greek culture still play a large part in their identity. This means they are not willing to give up claims to having roots in the ancient Macedonia where Alexander grew up and ruled. In this part of the world, where turmoil seems never-ending, the existence of two Macedonias, one north and one south, poses huge questions. These questions–particularly those of what defines the true Macedonia, who Macedonia belongs to, and most significantly, who the "real" Macedonians are–have caused raging debate and political maneuverings for decades and probably will for some time to come.

Judging Alexander

Few figures in history have inspired more debate and controversy than Alexander the Great. Two of his generals, Ptolemy and Aristobulus, wrote firsthand accounts of his deeds, but these were later lost. Not a single document from Alexander's time remains.

The first written history of Alexander's life to survive, *Library of History* by Diodorus Siculus, was not published until nearly three centuries after his death. A second book, *History of Alexander* by Quintus Curtius Rufus, was published in the first century C.E. Arrian's *The Anabasis of Alexander* and Plutarch's *Life of Alexander* were both published in the second century C.E. *The Romance of Alexander the Great* by Pseudo-Callisthenes was published in the third century. These early histories, the basis for many subsequent books about the great conqueror's life, were themselves based on Ptolemy's and Aristobulus's accounts, as well as on stories that had been passed down verbally by people who knew Alexander or by people who had learned about him through second- or third-hand knowledge.

Many of those who have told Alexander's story have been biased, slanting or exaggerating the truth sometimes for and sometimes against him. While the broader picture of his conquests and some of the facts of his background and life are confirmed, many more facts and details will never be known with any certainty.

Alexander the Great has been considered both a god and a saint. Some believed he had divine powers. Paintings have depicted him wearing a halo. On the other hand, priests of the Zoroastrian faith, Persia's dominant religion before Alexander's conquests, demonized Alexander. Their legends paint him as one of the worst sinners in history.

Arabs, who came to know him as Iskander, described him as a kind of bogeyman. Coins that depicted Alexander wearing two rams' horns,

What Alexander Would Control Today
The shaded area shows how Alexander's empire at its height touches on what is now more than dozen countries in Western Europe, the Middle East, and Asia.

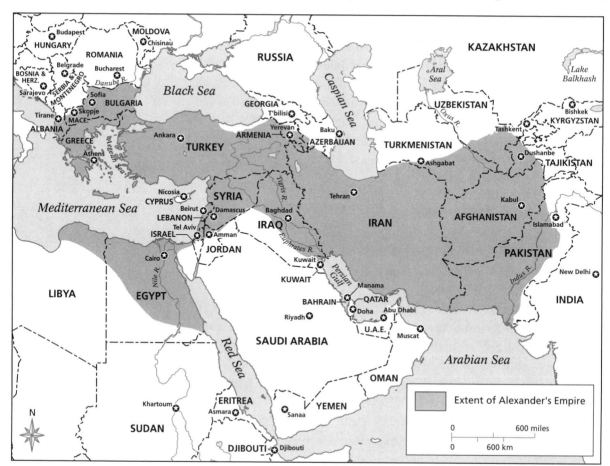

symbolizing the god Ammon, led later generations to believe he actually had horns. Even the Quran, the Muslim holy book, refers to him as Dhuyl Quarnein, or the "two-horned one."

The Greek city-states, his unwilling allies to whom he sent a fortune in war spoils, considered him a tyrant and rejoiced when he died.

Many critics have painted Alexander as an alcoholic. Supporters have defended his heavy drinking as the customary practice of his times.

Critics have reviled him for the brutality of some of his battles and the cruel murder and enslavement of some of his victims, including women and children. Supporters point to the fact that he did not allow his soldiers to rape women in lands they conquered and that he often pardoned enemies who surrendered as evidence of a noble character. Some historians salute him as an enlightened leader because he tried to unite all his subjects and to treat all races as equals. Others believe he abused his power, killing his detractors and demanding that people worship him.

That Alexander was one of the greatest military commanders of all time is one fact historians do not dispute. He never lost a major battle. Both Julius Caesar and Napoleon looked up to him as the ideal of a military leader. The young Macedonian king was also a great explorer. In this role, he established the limits of what was considered the inhabited earth. He opened up both sea and land routes that connected separate parts of the world for the first time. It was not until the voyages of the Portuguese and Spanish in the late 15th century that Europeans finally explored farther than Alexander had.

In judging Alexander the conqueror, it is important to consider the historical and cultural context of his life. Although today we consider the invasion of another country to be a crime, the idea that waging war is morally evil was not introduced until the beginning of the 19th century. During Alexander's times, invading and taking over another country was not rare nor even considered wrong. In fact, it was expected of a king.

As perhaps the most powerful leader of all antiquity, Alexander the Great more than fulfilled those expectations. Since the time of his own life, his contradictory personality—his extremes of valor, violence, and generosity—has riveted the attention of those who try to understand the man behind the master military general. The glory and ferocity of his acts still echo down the centuries. Alexander the Great remains as fascinating in modern times as he was 2,000 years ago.

TIME LINE

356 B.C.E.	Alexander is born in Pella, Macedonia.
338 B.C.E.	King Philip of Macedonia conquers Athens and Thebes in the battle of Chaeronaea, in which Alexander commands the left flank of the army.
336 B.C.E.	King Philip is murdered. Alexander succeeds to the throne of Macedonia.
335 B.C.E.	Alexander destroys the Greek city of Thebes as punishment for its revolt.
334 B.C.E.	Alexander invades Asia Minor. Alexander defeats King Darius III at the Battle of the Granicus River.
333 B.C.E.	Alexander defeats Darius III at the Battle of Issus.
332 B.C.E.	Alexander conquers Tyre after a seven-month siege.
331 B.C.E.	Egypt surrenders to Alexander and crowns him pharoah. Alexander establishes the city of Alexandria. Alexander defeats Darius III at the Battle of Gaugamela. Alexander is hailed as King of Persia.
330 B.C.E.	Darius III is murdered by his own troops.
330–327 B.C.E.	Alexander conquers eastern Persia.
326 B.C.E.	Alexander invades India.
	Alexander defeats King Porus at the Battle of Hydaspes. Alexander's troops refuse to continue, forcing him to return to Persia.
324 B.C.E.	Alexander organizes a mass marriage at Susa, and marries his second and third wives.
	Alexander's closest friend, Hephaestion, dies in Persia.
323 B.C.E.	Alexander dies in Babylon on June 10, at the age of 32. A power struggle erupts for control of his kingdom.
	Alexander the Great's son with his first wife, Roxane, is born shortly after his father's death. He is also named Alexander.
310 B.C.E.	Cassander, the new king of Macedonia, executes Roxane and Alexander's son, who is 13 years old.

RESOURCES: Books

Chrisp, Peter. *Alexander the Great: The Legend of a Warrior King* (New York: DK Publishing, 2000)

This book follows the history of Alexander the Great and his campaign to conquer the known world, including information on his traveling companions, armies of his time, ships, and food. There are a lot of illustrations and factoids.

Greenblatt, Miriam. *Alexander the Great and Ancient Greece.* (Tarrytown, N.Y.: Benchmark Books, 2000)

This short book is divided into two main sections. The first provides a brief history of Alexander and his conquests. The second describes everyday life in ancient Greece.

Harris, Nathaniel. *Alexander the Great and the Greeks.* (East Sussex, UK: Wayland Publishers, Ltd., 1985)

An extremely easy-to-read short book that focuses primarily on Greek culture. It also tells the story of Alexander the Great's conquests very briefly.

Nardo, Don, *The Persian Empire.* (San Diego, Calif.: Lucent Books, 1998)

This book provides a history of the Persian Empire and its people from ancient to modern times. It is broken up into short, readable sections and sidebars, with a section on Alexander the Great.

Robinson, Charles Alexander, Jr. *Alexander the Great.* (New York: Franklin Watts, 1963)

This is a well-written account of Alexander's life, career, and influence. The book provides a balanced view of historical events, with insightful analysis.

Theule, Frederic. *Alexander and His Times* (New York: Henry Holt and Company, 1995)

Magazine-like graphics make this book easy to read. Well-documented research is presented in a fun and imaginative way.

Wepman, Dennis. *Alexander the Great* (Philadelphia: Chelsea House Publishers, 1986)

This book, part of the series World Leaders Past & Present, is an account of Alexander's life and times. It is highly readable and contains a lot of sidebars, photographs, and illustrations.

RESOURCES: Web Sites

Alexander Changes the World
www.fsmitha.com/h1/ch11.htm
> This web site provides a narrative history from historian Frank E. Smitha of Antiquity Online. Maps and links to other Alexander the Great sites are included. Opinions are explicitly labeled as such.

Alexander the Great
www.hackneys.com/alex_web/index.htm
> This web site was created by three high school freshmen for the Wisconsin state history project competition in 1997. Authors Adam Hackney, John Eifealdt, and Jeremy Tilsen, from Hudson High School in Hudson, Wisconsin, continue to maintain and update the site. it is highly readable and well organized, and contains articles on each of Alexander's battles, as well as overviews of many aspects of Alexander's life and a glossary.

Alexander the Great's Home on the Web
www.pothos.org
> This comprehensive web site was created by Thomas William-Powlett, a former educator. Other authors contribute articles to the site, which is maintained by a team of volunteers. When it was launched in 1994, it was the first web site dedicated to Alexander the Great. It contains book reviews, articles, timelines, and a trivia quiz.

Alexander the Great on the Web
www.isidore-of-seville.com/Alexanderama.html
> This site, edited by Tim Spaulding, is a web directory of information about Alexander the Great. It provides exhaustive lists of and links to biographies, articles, papers, books, movies, television programs, maps, images, and more. There are notes and short reviews about each resource.

Ancient Persia
members.ozemail.com.au/~ancientpersia/index.html
> This site, by Mark Drury, contains information about ancient Persia. It focuses on the Archaemenid Empire.

Encarta
encarta.msn.com
> A search on "Alexander the Great" on this on-line encyclopedia site results in a number of listings. Some articles can only be accessed by subscribers, but a number of the articles are available to the public.

Livius Articles on Ancient History
www.livius.org/aj-al/alexander/alexander00.html
> This extremely comprehensive site includes 18 in-depth articles covering the life of Alexander chronologically. Each article has links to deeper levels of details, and there is a comprehensive index. The site explores history from both the Greek and Persian perspectives, drawing on 70 ancient sources. It was developed by educator Jona Lendering from Amsterdam.

BIBLIOGRAPHY

"Alexander the Great." Encarta Online Encyclopedia. URL: http://encarta.msn.com/encnet/refpages/SRPage.aspx?search=alexander+the+great&Submit2=Go. Updated 2004.

"Alexander the Great: The Romance of Alexander." The 1911 Edition Encyclopedia Online. URL: http://47.1911encyclopedia.org/A/AL/ALEXANDER_THE_GREAT.htm. Updated 2003.

"Antiqua Medicina From Homer to Vesalius: Alexandrian Medicine–The Alexandrian School." University of Virginia Medical School. URLs: http://www.med.virginia.edu/hs-library/historical/antiqua/anthome.html; http://www.med.virginia.edu/hs-library/historical/antiqua/stexta.htm; http://www.med.virginia.edu/hs-library/historical/antiqua/textd.htm. Updated July 2003.

Arrian (translated by Aubrey de Sélincourt), *The Campaigns of Alexander.* New York: Viking Penguin, 1982.

"Ballista." Wikipedia. URL: http://en.wikipedia.org/wiki/Ballista. Updated June 13, 2004.

"Battleship." Encyclopædia Britannica Online. URL: http://search.eb.com/eb/article?eu=13962. Updated 2004.

The Bible, authorized King James version. Oxford, U.K.: Oxford University Press, 1992.

Bienkowski, Piotr, and Millard, Alan, *Dictionary of the Ancient Near East.* Philadelphia: University of Pennsylvania Press, 2000.

Borza, Eugene N., ed., *The Impact of Alexander the Great.* Hinsdale, Ill.: The Dryden Press, 1974.

"Catapult." Wikipedia. URL: http://en.wikipedia.org/wiki/Catapult. Updated June 28, 2004.

Cotterell, Arthur, ed., *The Penguin Encyclopedia of Classical Civilizations.* Middlesex, U.K.: The Penguin Group, 1993.

Cowan, Ross, *Roman Legionary, 58 B.C.–A.D. 69.* Oxford and London, U.K.: Osprey Publishing, 2003.

"Dreadnought." Encyclopædia Britannica Online. URL: http://search.eb.com/eb/article?eu=31678. Updated 2004.

Fox, Robin Lane, *Alexander the Great.* London: Penguin Books, 1973.

"The Greek Language." Translexis Limited. URL: http://www.translexis.demon.co.uk/new_page_2.htm. Posted 2002.

Hayes, Carlton J.H., *Ancient Civilizations: Prehistory to the Fall of Rome.* New York: MacMillan Publishing Co., 1983.

Herodotus (translated by Aubrey de Sélincourt), *The Histories.* New York: Penquin Classics, 1972.

Joshi, Sopan, "Where on Earth? The Gwadar Enclave." *Outlook Traveler Magazine.* URL: http://www.outlooktraveller.com/asp-scripts/mag_art.asp?magid=212&p. Posted December 2001.

Lendering, Jona, ed., "Livius: Articles on Ancient History." URL: http://www.livius.org/greece.html. Accessed May 28, 2004.

"Macedonia." Encyclopædia Britannica Online. URL: http://search.eb.com/ebi/article?eu=297567; http://search.eb.com/ebi/article?eu=297568; http://search.eb.com/eb/article?eu=119675; http://search.eb.com/eb/article?eu=119677; http://search.eb.com/eb/article?eu=50900; http://search.eb.com/eb/article?eu=50901; http://search.eb.com/eb/article?eu=50902. Updated 2004.

Meyers, Eric M., ed., *The Oxford Encyclopedia of Archeology in the Near East.* New York: Oxford University Press, 1997.

"A Monumental Building in a City of Magnificent Intentions." Office of the Curator, Department of the Treasury Exhibition–Greek Revival Architecture in Washington, D.C. URL: http://www.ustreas.gov/offices/management/curator/exhibitions/2002exhibit/greekrevival.html. Posted 2002.

"Naval Ship." Encyclopædia Britannica Online. URL: http://search.eb.com/eb/article?eu=118842; http://search.eb.com/eb/article?eu=118843. Updated 2004.

"Pasni, Pakistan: 25°17'17.23"N 63°20'37.76"E." Global Security. URL: http://www.globalsecurity.org/military/facility/pasni.htm. Updated September 27, 2002.

Pseudo-Callisthenes (translated by Richard Stoneman), *The Greek Alexander Romance.* New York. Penguin, 1991.

Rahnamoon, Fariborz, "History of Persian or Parsi Language." Iran Chamber Society. URL: http://www.iranchamber.com/literature/articles/persian_parsi_language_history.php. Updated 2004.

Ramet, Ph.D., Sabrina P., "Macedonia." Chicago: World Book Encyclopedia Interactive CD, 2004 edition.

Renault, Mary, *The Nature of Alexander.* New York: Pantheon Books, 1975.

Sadek, Samir, "The Mouseion Revisited."Al-Ahram Weekly Online (No. 668). URL: http://weekly.ahram.org.eg/2003/668/hel.htm. Published December 11–17, 2003.

Sekunda, Nick, *Republican Roman Army, 200–104 B.C.* Oxford and London, U.K.: Osprey Publishing, 1999.

"Spices: Exotic Flavors and Medicines." UCLA History and Special Collections, Louise M. Darling Biomedical Library. URL: http://unitproj.library.ucla.edu/biomed/spice/. Posted 2002.

Vlamis, Christos Thomas, ed., "Arachaeonia: A Journey Through Ancient Greece." URL: http://archaeonia.com. Updated June 4, 2003.

Wallace, Daniel B., *Greek Grammar Beyond the Basics.* Grand Rapids, Mich.: Zondervan, 1996.

Welles, C. Bradford, *Alexander and the Hellenistic World.* Toronto, Ontario.: A.M. Hakkert, Ltd., 1970.

Welman, Nick, "All About Alexander the Great." Pothos.org. URL: http://www.pothos.org/alexander.asp?paraID=78&keyword_id=8&title=Army. Accessed July 23, 2004.

Whitehouse, David, "Library of Alexandria Discovered."BBC News, UK Edition Online. URL: http://news.bbc.co.uk/1/hi/sci/tech/3707641.stm. Posted May 12, 2004.

Wood, Michael, *In the Footsteps of Alexander the Great: A Journey from Greece to Asia.* Berkeley and Los Angeles, Calif.: University of California Press, 1997.

Worthington, Ian, ed., *Alexander the Great: A Reader.* London and New York: Routledge, 2003.

INDEX

Page numbers in *italics* refer to illustration captions.